VALENTINO
ROSSI

THIRD EDITION

VALENTINO

ROSSI

MotoGenius

MAT OXLEY

Haynes Publishing

First published in hardback in 2002
Reprinted in 2002 (twice)
Second edition published in 2003
This third edition, reformatted with additional material,
published in paperback in 2005

A catalogue record for this book is
available from the British Library

ISBN 1 84425 217 5

Library of Congress catalog card no. 2004 117158

Published by Haynes Publishing, Sparkford,
Yeovil, Somerset, BA22 7JJ, UK
Tel: 01963 442030 Fax: 01963 440001
Int.tel: +44 1963 442030 Int.fax: +44 1963 440001
E-mail: sales@haynes.co.uk
Website: www.haynes.co.uk

Haynes North America, Inc.,
861 Lawrence Drive, Newbury Park,
California 91320, USA

Designed and typeset by G&M Designs Limited,
Raunds, Northamptonshire
Printed and bound in England by
J. H. Haynes & Co. Ltd, Sparkford

CONTENTS

For Bill Brightman
One of Valentino's biggest, littlest fans

ACKNOWLEDGEMENTS

Big thanks to Valentino and everyone else who helped with this book. All these and more: Aprilia, Luigino 'Gibo' Badioli, Max Biaggi, Rossano Brazzi, Jerry Burgess, Barry Coleman, Mick Doohan, Carlo Fiorani, Rossana Fuzzi, Gold and Goose, Mark Graham, Ross Holleron, Honda Racing Corporation, Hamish Jamieson, Eva Jirsenska, Henk Keulemans, Mac Mackay, Niall Mackenzie, Elena Manzoni, Charlotte Menard, *Motosprint*, Elena Radina, Dr Martin Raines, Wayne Rainey, Kenny Roberts, Graziano Rossi, Stefania Rossi, Giampiero Sacchi, Stefano Saragoni, Kevin Schwantz, Michael Scott, Gigi Soldano, Koji Sugita, Hidenobu Takeuchi, Chris Walker, Warren Willing and Debbie van Zon.

FOREWORD
to the second edition

by Mick Doohan
500 World Champion 1994–1998

Valentino continues to surprise me. More than anything, it's his mental strength. He's got the capability to stay right on it week after week, which is where the other guys fall short. For sure he's fast, but some of the others are fast too. It's his mental strength that pulls him through. If ever he has a problem and a little doubt creeps in, he pulls through and he's stronger than before.

Ever since he's been in GPs he's been good for the sport. He's a colourful character, he loves life, he loves riding motorcycles and he wants to portray that to everybody. He arrived and changed the way people think about racing. He proved that you can have fun, even though he's very serious and focused.

Also, he's a team player. He doesn't believe he's the only guy in the team and that's really important in racing. Sure, he's lucky to have Jeremy Burgess and the team working with him, like I was – because JB's got so much experience – but he has got a very good feeling for the motorcycle. He understands what's going on around him, which is why he tends to stay on. A lot of guys feel what's going on but they don't know how to translate the feeling to their engineers.

Valentino is at a point in his career where he's been thinking about getting into car racing. The biggest factor in his future is going to be how long he wants to continue riding and this is an issue that Valentino alone will determine.

I've known author Mat Oxley even longer than I've known Valentino, since I first came to GPs in '89. That season was a bit of a struggle for me, but Mat was one guy who kept writing that I might have some ability long-term. Since then he's become one of the most respected media guys in the paddock. He tells things like they are; he's a straight-shooter. He'll give praise when it's deserved and criticise when it's warranted. As a rider, you can't ask for more than that.

Gold Coast, Australia

INTRODUCTION

Motorcycle racing is a funny old game. In fact it is *the* funny old game of 'I can go faster than you' amplified to the nth degree; grown men risking life and limb for ego.

This book is about a man who has played this game like few others, achieving an extraordinary run of successes while wearing a smile as wide as his extravagant racing lines. Valentino Rossi just loves racing motorcycles, and his infectious enthusiasm for speed and two wheels has transported him into the mainstream and helped change the way the world looks at bike racing. As someone recently said, Rossi is not your 'typical motorcycle racing psychopath'.

Valentino skipped into the World Championship arena nine years ago as a mopheaded teenager. 'Who's that girl?' people asked. Now, as an afro-haired London geezer, his face is more recognised than any motorcyclist's in history. Rossi has become GP racing, he's a phenomenon, and yet he's a rider on a multi-million pound salary who still likes to muck about with the stickers on his race bike. That's not normal.

Valentino keeps it simple, stays true to his roots. He's a rider who thinks deeply about his racing but never out-thinks himself. His philosophy is straightforward: think hard, have fun. He isn't a desperate trier, he's a natural, doing the right thing comes easily to him, whether it's riding right or looking right. The man understands.

He approaches his racing both as boy and man, both as art and science. To him the art of the racing line is 'like a poem', which is why he can magic the kind of lines of which most racers seem incapable. As paddock philosopher Dr Claudio

Costa says: 'Valentino abandons himself to the creativity of the mind so that he can play the game of life according to the carefree rules of the child.'

And yet he is almost digitally efficient. 'The weirdest thing that happens to me when I'm racing,' he says, 'is that I perceive the race not as a unit but as a succession of fragments that pass before my eyes in slow motion.' Which may go some way to explaining how he unerringly applied his relentless two-year programme to deal with the 125, 250 and 500 World Championships; one year to explore each new class, one year to conquer. But in 2002 he ditched the two-year plan, dominating the new four-stroke MotoGP class from the outset. And last year he achieved, if not the impossible, the improbable by winning the title at his first attempt on the unfancied Yamaha M1. His touch, it seems, is more golden than that of King Midas.

Valentino is so good at racing, so good at life, that he seems almost too good to be true, like the invention of some Hollywood scriptwriter with a Superman complex who writes an impossible amount of genius and nobility into his male lead. Of course, Rossi isn't Superman, he just likes to dress that way sometimes.

Mat Oxley
London, England, Spring 2005

Chapter 1

IL FENOMENO ROSSI

Rossi mania grabbed me for the first time during the 1979 British GP at Silverstone. Standing at Stowe Corner amongst the crumpled beer cans, I watched Graziano Rossi lay waste to the 250 pack, his extravagant style and the speed of his lovely Morbidelli moving him well clear of that year's World Champ, Kawasaki's Kork Ballington. With just three corners to go he had stretched his advantage to an unbeatable 2.5 seconds. Then he crashed.

As a reckless 20-year-old I thought that was pretty cool – chucking away a surefire win like he just didn't care. Why slow down just because you can almost taste the champagne? Rossi was a motorcycle racer doing what he thought he was paid to do: going as fast as he possibly could, from green light to chequered flag. Silverstone should've been his fourth win of the year, instead it was the last time he got close to winning a grand prix.

Papa Rossi also looked pretty damn fly, like Jesus, only much faster. His leathers and helmet were white, rent through by a zigzag lightning streak of red and green for the Italian tricolor, and his shoulder-length hair whipped around from beneath his helmet. But it wasn't a dodgy haircut, Rossi was way too cool, way too charismatic, to ever look wrong. In fact, he was so right that I used to spend evenings doing sketches of my own Rossi-replica leathers and helmet, which I kind of knew I'd never get around to owning.

Rossi retired a few years later, a nasty bump on the head forcing an end to a career that never made the most of his intelligence and riding talent. He faded from my memory after I started racing, still without those red, white and green leathers. Twelve years later I spotted him off a bike for the first time, not counting that moment he'd parted company with his Morbidelli at Silverstone. During the summer of '91 I was in the Adriatic resort of Rimini doing a story on Italy's latest craze, minimoto racing, and there he was, stood by the track beneath the floodlights (it was almost midnight), watching intently. I went over to shake his hand, to tell him he'd been a hero of mine and to ask him what he was doing at some dodgy minimoto track in the middle of the night. Rossi pointed into the gloom, at a midget figure circulating the midget racetrack on a midget bike. 'Is my son, Valentino,' he grinned. 'Good to meet you,' I replied, and not wanting to cause any further embarrassment to either of us, I made my excuses and left papa and bambino to themselves, never thinking I'd see them again.

Of course, I got to see plenty of them, we all did. Over the next decade the little kid would grow into a big kid, dazzling pretty much the whole world with his speed and charisma, his ever so slightly eccentric dad along for the ride, eschewing flash hotels to sleep in the back of his BMW.

It wouldn't be too much of an exaggeration to say that Valentino Rossi has changed the face of grand prix racing; certainly no other bike racer has ever got closer to being a pop star. And his actual racing achievements are awe-inspiring, history-making stuff: first GP win at the age of 17, first world title at 18, another title at 20, his first 500 win a few months after his 21st birthday, the final 500 World Championship a year later and the first three MotoGP crowns in 2002, 2003 and 2004. Last year's success, achieved very much against the odds on Yamaha's much-maligned M1, also included the first back-to-back premier-class wins on different makes of machinery in the sport's 55-year history. He's also the fourth youngest rider to have worn the premier-class crown, the youngest man to have won six world titles and at the age of just 26 he's already in the top five of the all-time GP winners' list.

His progress has been so relentless that it smacks of the automaton sportsman – grim-faced, head down, no thought for anything but total victory – and yet each and every one of his successes has been achieved with a joy that never fails to touch everyone's heart. 'Valentino likes to win, he's a great fighter,' says his engineer Jeremy Burgess, who's worked closely with the youngster since the end of 1999. 'But he also knows we're in the entertainment business, so he likes to entertain.'

Even back in his 125 and 250 days his infectious enthusiasm was breaking the sport to whole new audiences, amongst them the Valenteenyboppers, gangs of Italian schoolgirls drawn to racetracks by their heart-throb's pretty blue eyes. Valentino doesn't appreciate that kind of attention though because he's a bit of a biking purist. 'They're not fans of Rossi the motorcycle racer, but just because I've got blue eyes, I don't like,' he says with faint exasperation after years spent fleeing these seething ranks of moist, pubescent Latin lovelies. 'It's good to have one or two nice girls chasing you, but not one thousand.' That's what he says, but you wonder if he really means it once you've been inside his motorhome, watching him and constant companion Uccio Salucci giggling madly as they field lewd text messages from female admirers.

For all his talent and his charm Rossi is a sponsors' darling, and yet he stays true to himself, tells it like it is, he doesn't do PR spew. Like he's never afraid to voice his dislike of bitter rivals Max Biaggi and Sete Gibernau and that's something in GP racing, where everyone has got into the habit of 'sugaring each others' asses', as former 500 champ King Kenny Roberts once put it.

Valentino knows how to make people laugh too. Perhaps his cheesiest post-race celebrations have been a mite overdone but he was pure comedy at Jerez '99, dumping his Aprilia

RSW250 halfway around the victory lap and diving into a marshals' trackside Portaloo, emerging seconds later to 150,000 fans going off their nuts.

So what has he got that other racers haven't? He's a phenomenon, the leader of a new breed of cool GP racer, a bright, enlightened 21st century version of the macho hell-raisers of old. Maybe there's never been a rider who combines such warmth of character with so much natural talent, raw bravery and tireless dedication.

To dissect and understand the Rossi phenomenon we should begin by looking further back than his immediate genes. We must look to where he comes from, because his national culture is just as important as his inherited family characteristics. Italy is the heart and soul of motorsport, Italians are obsessed with speed, and when it comes to racing as romance, they're the kings, from Ducati to Ferrari, from Agostini to Nuvolari, from Monza to the Mille Miglia.

Italy's record of bike racing glory is beyond compare. During 55 years of motorcycle grand prix racing, Italian riders have scored more than twice as many 125, 250, 500 and MotoGP victories as any other nation. By the end of the 2003 season Italians had won 554 GPs, the British are next with 276 victories, then the Spanish (185), the Americans (169) and the Japanese (154).

Valentino is just the latest in a long lineage of racetrack conquerors that goes way back to the pre-war exploits of Tazio Nuvolari (the grand prix car legend who started out on bikes) and thence to 1950 500 World Champion Umberto Maseti, Sixties' and Seventies' heroes Giacomo Agostini, Walter Villa and Renzo Pasolini, Eighties' 500 World Champions Marco Lucchinelli and Franco Uncini, and current names like Biaggi, Loris Capirossi and Marco Melandri.

So from where do the Italians get their lust for speed, what are its roots? Their passion goes back to the start of the 20th century, to the earliest days of the motor industry when Italy fell head over heels in love with the machine and the future that machines might offer. Futurism was an Italian cultural phenomenon, fuelled by the birth of the new technological society, a new age of noise and speed: aeroplanes, cars, motorcycles and telecommunications. 'We declare that the world's splendour has been enriched by a new beauty: the beauty of speed,' proclaimed Italy's 1909 manifesto of Futurism. 'A racing motor car, its frame adorned with great pipes, like snakes with explosive breath ... a roaring motor car, which seems to run on shrapnel ...' Okay, so they were getting a bit carried away but you can see what they meant, and it's no different now; in Britain people hate noisy cars and bikes, in Italy they love 'em.

Officially sanctioned long-distance street races, roaring from one town to the next, exploded across Italy during the 1920s as the nation's big five motorcycle factories (the so-called Pentarchia of Benelli, Bianchi, Garelli, Gilera and Guzzi) fought for supremacy in the showrooms by fighting for supremacy on the 'racetracks'. Such was the national passion for these often lethal events that Italy was the last Continental nation to ban racing on public roads. Italy's powered two-wheeler industry really took off after the Second World War when the rapidly industrialising nation needed to get the largely peasant workforce out of the villages and into the factories. The workers required transport but cars were beyond their meagre wages, so the scooter was born. Lambretta and Vespa were both established in 1946, and four years later Ducati and Aermacchi joined the race for mobilisation.

As sales boomed, so did the race scene. Most of the manufacturers were enthusiastic in their involvement and they naturally signed up local riders who could communicate with their engineers and promote sales in the all-important home market, as Biaggi and Rossi did so well for Aprilia half a century later. (It is no coincidence that the vast majority of Britain's 276 GP successes were achieved when the country had a motorcycle industry.)

It is more difficult to ponder exactly when the Italians first fell in love with engineering and maybe it would be pushing the point to speculate that the first sparks were ignited by Leonardo da Vinci and the Renaissance way back in the 15th and 16th centuries. Or maybe not, for Italy has been renowned for its artisans ever since. The metal workers who toiled at Enzo Ferrari's first workshops, for example, were craftsmen continuing Modena's centuries-old reputation for skilled manufacture of just about anything in metal. Of course, there are other less complex reasons for Italy's ongoing motorcycling success story, like the fact that the sun shines a whole lot more down there than it does in northern Europe.

Whatever, Valentino's Italian blood is a major factor in his success, in all kinds of ways. He has that Latin lust for life and a sunny, catholic attitude, he's enthusiastic, loquacious and determined to have fun, even though he's involved in a deadly serious business. His attitude to life and to racing demands inevitable comparisons with that of Mick Doohan, the man who dominated 500 GPs when Valentino was riding 125s and 250s, and whose team he inherited after the Australian quit racing at the end of 1999.

In fact, 'The Doctor' and 'Mighty Mick' have little in common, apart from their blinding talent to ride a motorcycle faster than anyone else on this planet. Doohan was a driven man, to the scariest of degrees, he used to go racing like there were demons chasing him, and if he ever slowed down, they'd have him. There was a terrorised urgency to his riding, he forced the bike down into corners, hunched over the front like some kind of desperado; 'all prick and ribs like a drover's dog', as the Aussies would say. Who knows what drove him, but the inside of a racer's head is a strange place: weird forces driving weird psyches to take weird risks, and maybe the pain that cut right through his injury-blighted career coloured his temperament. Valentino (so far, touch wood, relatively unscarred by racing) doesn't seem to possess that kind of mildly psychotic inner self and really does look like he's having fun on the bike; he looks more natural, more fluid, more smooth. Off track he appears remarkably well adjusted, with few obvious signs of that often ruinous desperation to prove himself bigger and braver than everyone else, which is the defining behavioural characteristic of so many racers. Mostly he just seems to be having a ball.

'I've always said Mick enjoyed winning and Valentino enjoys racing,' adds Burgess, who previously guided Doohan to his five 500 crowns. 'If Valentino has a great race and finishes second, he's disappointed but he's not angry with the world like Mick used to be, he's not going to tear your head off.'

Former journalist Barry Coleman, who covered the World Championships when Rossi senior was racing, knows from where he got those characteristics. 'Graziano was anything but a typical motorcycle racing psychopath,' Coleman recalls. 'He's a marvellous man and it's inevitable that Valentino has taken a lot from having a dad like that. Valentino recently said: "I'm just a fan on a bike", and I think that's exactly how he is.'

Too true, Vale (as mates call him, pronounced 'Valay') was a dedicated GP anorak long before he started racing, with an encyclopaedic knowledge of riders' helmet designs, numbers and liveries. One of his earliest visits to a GP is burned into his memory, as it would be in the mind of any ordinary race fan. 'The first GP I remember going to see was Mugello '91,' he says. 'I used to watch all the races on TV, so I knew all the riders' numbers, all their helmet designs, the whole circus. I was with Gibo (Badioli, old family friend and now his manager) and Graziano. We parked the camper at Casanova Savelli (a daunting, downhill right–left flick where his fan club now camps out) and I remember very well the 125 race with Ueda, with number 56 and the green and blue Hero Sports Honda, fighting with Capirossi and Gresini.' This is not normal. Most riders hold zero interest in other racers, except their direct competitors, but Valentino really is an enthusiast. He can even recognise a journalist's helmet design. When I was researching this book he grabbed my lid and said: 'Yes, I remember your helmet from when I was a boy reading *Motosprint* [Italy's biking weekly], didn't you have a big accident one day, going under a truck?' Well, yes, I did. So what can we tell from this? That he's bright, that he's got a good memory, but most of all that he's interested in ordinary people, which is a serious rarity in the me-me-me world of GP racing. Some top-line racers show less interest in people like us than some folk might in their dustman.

He is even aware that it was pretty weird having the first edition of his biography published when he was 23 (in fact this was the fourth Rossi book in as many summers). 'Yes,' he grins. 'Is strange, but I don't take it serious, it's not possible to take everything serious, in life or in racing. If possible I take it with a smile, it makes life easier.'

Valentino's uncomplicated, unaffected, unpretentious attitude to life and racing is everything. Nowadays, GPs are more intense, if less lethal, than they've ever been. Track safety may be better than ever but the danger is still there, and grand prix riders tend to crash more often these days, because the demands and rewards of World Championship racing drive them to exist on the outer extremes of traction. Some crashes hurt more than others; very few don't hurt at all. Highsides (racing's equivalent of flinging yourself out of a speeding express train) hardly ever happen without a subsequent visit to Dr Claudio Costa's Clinica Mobile for a dose of mesotherapy, a local pain-relief therapy that can require more than 100 micro-injections. As Valentino says: 'I have very much fear of the mesotherapy needle. Of course, I'm scared about getting hurt, but what am I going to do, lock myself in a room and be happy being safe?'

The further psychological pressures on top riders are crushing, impossible to overestimate, and come from every direction – from the factory, from the sponsors, from the team, from the media, from the fans and, of course, from inside the rider himself. Sure, there's harder ways to make a living, but when these guys aren't on the bike they're huddled for hours in debriefing sessions with their engine, chassis and tyre engineers, surrounded by the flicker of computer monitors and the whirr-whirr of hard drives. And if they're not doing that, they're being gushed over by their sponsors, suffocated by the fans or harangued by the media. Racing becomes a chore.

Which is why so many modern-day riders are anything but a bundle of laughs. In TV interviews they stare at the camera, mouthing weary platitudes because their minds are burdened by some hi-tech conundrum: transient engine behaviour, high-speed rebound damping curves and data-logging outputs. Valentino seems to be one of the few top guys who has this sorted. By keeping the joy, he rides at his very best. He rides fast because he wants to, because it's a blast. Many of his rivals have let the serious stuff get to them, so they've stopped having fun, so they struggle to be as quick, week in, week out.

Back in bike racing's so-called golden days – the Fifties, Sixties and Seventies – GP racers were fast-living, up-for-a-laugh daredevils, apparently able to win races with inspired, risk-taking heroics. Back then racing was an art and racers behaved accordingly: out on the piss, sniffing and snorting their way through ranks of glamorous shags.

It's not like that anymore. Racing at grand prix level is now a science and racers are the front-line laboratory troops, they just wear leathers instead of white lab coats. It's not only about white-knuckle, devil-may-care risk taking anymore, nowadays racing is a cold and precise science – a giant, globally televised physics experiment. Sure, racers need balls just as much as they ever did, but only as much as they need to understand the science of it all. Sixties' legend Mike Hailwood, who like Valentino won his first 500 crown at the age of 22, was happily technophobic. Vale may not be a rocket scientist but he needs to be able to discuss deep technical concepts with his crew for hours and hours. As King Kenny Roberts puts it: 'People say the riders aren't the same fun guys they used to be, well, they don't have the time to be, that's the whole thing.'

There is a parallel here with the USAF's jet-fighter test pilots, as described in Hunter S. Thompson's book *The Great Shark Hunt*. The gun totin', acid casualty author talks of how, during the Sixties, the USAF developed 'a computerised version of the legendary, hell-for-leather test pilot', banishing the old 'kick the tyre, light the fire and away we go' heroes of old. He goes on: 'the best pilot in the world – even if he could land a B-52 on the number eight green at Pebble Beach without taking a divot – would be useless on a test-flight project unless he could explain, in a written report, just how and why the landing could be made.'

It's the same with modern racers – GP bikes are so hi-tech that riders must be able to describe machine behaviour in acute detail, then analyse potential improvements with their technicians. And there's another link between old fliers and GP racers. Thompson describes how USAF test pilots used to get their off-duty kicks on terra firma around their base in the Mojave desert: 'back in the good old days, when men were men and might was right and the devil took the hindmost, the peaceful desert highways were raceways for off-duty pilots on big motorcycles. Slow-moving travellers were frequently blown off the road by wildmen in leather jackets and white scarves, human torpedoes defying all speed limits and heedless of their own safety.'

Not any more, when he revisited the base years later Thompson found the USAF appalled at the idea of anything as fun and as dangerous as a motorcycle. 'Today's pilots go to bed early, and regard big motorcycles with the same analytical disdain they have for hippies, winos and other failure symbols. They take their risks, on assignment, between dawn and 4.30pm'. In GP racing, it's Sundays between noon and 3pm.

That's exactly what Valentino found when he came to GPs in 1996. If Doohan had raised dedication and commitment to a new level, the Australian's psychotic approach to racing had transformed paddock atmosphere. Mighty Mick was breaking everyone's balls (including his own), he brought withering aggression and unrelenting pressure to his racing, because that's what he needed to win. And he was so successful that everyone mimicked his attitude until the paddock became almost unbearably intense. Valentino wanted to change all that, he couldn't imagine going racing and not having fun, he'd hate it, what'd be the point? So he changed things.

'When I came to GPs all the riders were very, very serious,' he recalls. 'So when I started winning, me and my friends decided we should try to make some big fun. We just wanted to do something new to show the big emotion of winning races. The ideas usually came to us in a bar in Tavullia at two in the morning! They were just a game, just some fun with my fan club.'

From the Portaloo gag to the prank with the blow-up doll, through his entire alter ego wardrobe from Robin Hood to Superman, and through his numerous Madonna-like makeovers from girly mophead to bearded ragamuffin via skinhead and trance cadet, Valentino tells the world that he likes a laugh. It's all just good fun, though there's little doubt there's an element of palliative here, as if to ward off the round-the-clock stress that gets to many big-time riders. By halfway through a GP season some riders look burned out and ground down, but Valentino counteracts the pressure, even though, or perhaps because, he's the most sought after of all, his every step dogged by a ravenous pack of Italian media, shades on, notebooks in hand, pretending to be his mate.

No motorcycle racer has ever been bigger than Rossi, not even glam Seventies' superstar Barry Sheene who was famously namechecked in a top-ten hit. He is, if you like, the David Beckham of bikes and, like Becks, he pays a high price for his fame having crossed over into the mainstream. Like Becks and Andre Agassi, he's the guy who transcended his sport's own territory, because he doesn't only appeal to blokes. The ladies, the Valenteenies and the kids love him too; so these days whole families sit down to watch GP racing like never before.

Valentino arrived at the pinnacle of his sport with impeccable timing, for motorcycle racing needed someone with mainstream pulling power if it was to thrust itself into the global consciousness. Like any other 21st century sport, bike racing is a commodity that has to be sold to as many consumers as possible, and Valentino's sweet, smiling face is exactly what the sport, and the corporations behind it, were looking for, the weapon that would fire their products deep into the wish lists of consumers. Indeed, there've been times over the last few years when it appears that Rossi *is* grand prix racing, he is its sun, the rest of the MotoGP show just orbits around him.

As a result, his life is barely his own these days, indeed he is so popular at home that he's had to exile himself to London.

The pressures of celebrity really began to bite home as he strode towards the 500 title in 2001. Battered by the incessant demands of the media, his sweet nature hardened somewhat, the perma-grin of his 125 and 250 years buckled; it had to if he was to preserve his sanity. And he gave up his more outlandish post-race celebrations. This, after all, is what we do to the celebrities we adore. We squeeze out of them exactly what it is that we love within them, as Oscar Wilde once observed, we kill the things we love.

Even so, Valentino is still as at ease with his mind-boggling fame as it's possible to be. And in that sense he's the very opposite of his predecessor Doohan, who couldn't help but look agonisingly, but endearingly, awkward whenever thrust into the limelight outside of his helmet. Doohan, you see, never crossed into the mainstream, never ever wanted to. Roberts again: 'The things that make Valentino popular are also the things that make life hard for him. If you're only a good motorcycle racer it's one thing, but the more your face gets splashed around the place for selling sunglasses, watches and stuff like that, the more problems you're going to have. For every plus there's a minus, and the more pluses, the more minuses. That's the way the world works, we didn't invent it, we just have to live in it.'

The devastating demands of riding the fastest bikes on earth have also made their mark. Like Doohan, Eighties' 500 king Eddie Lawson and many others before him, Valentino's face has aged rapidly since he moved on from 250s: the cheeks more hollow, the eyes more sunken, the look a little more haunted. That's what 200 horsepower motorcycles do to you.

And yet despite the pressurised lifestyle, both on and off the track, he obviously does love what he's doing, and like Becks, he's fully aware of the Faustian contract he's made with fame. 'For sure there is more good than bad to being famous,' says Rossi with a glint in his eye. 'The bad thing is the stress. Now I can't go anywhere in the world without being recognised. Very many people recognise me and want autographs and photos. The situation is a little better in London but Italy is a nightmare, a nightmare, I will never be able to live a normal life there. Fame affects you in different ways; when you have many fans who follow you like a slipstream, yes, it's heavy, but it's good. But the Italian journalists only follow me for one reason, they're waiting for a mistake. If I say one word wrong or if I crash, it's 'Ah, fack, he's stupid!'. Fack? Yes, fack. Since he moved to London Vale has revealed a growing love for the 'F' word, delivered with an Italian intonation, like 'sack!'. The word obviously doesn't hold the same sting for him that it does for some uptight Anglo-Saxons; presumably it's the Latin derivative of the Gaelic 'Feck' …

Amidst the madness Valentino keeps it real by surrounding himself with mates, most of whom he's known since they got together to make some mischief in primary school. He doesn't do the celebrity circuit. His thick-as-thieves Latin homies call themselves the Tavullia Chihuahua (Tavullia, his hometown in Italy, the Chihuahua, a tribe of North American Indians), although, of course, this is only the inner sanctum; when Vale wrapped up the 2001 and 2004 500/MotoGP titles in Australia, thousands of Tavullians stayed up partying until 6am, watching the race on a big screen in the town piazza. No wonder he cherishes the anonymity of London.

Former 500 champion Kevin Schwantz, whom many older fans see as a kind of proto-Rossi because he shared a similar attitude to life and racing, remembers the stresses of racing being one of the hardest things to handle during his years at the top. 'I always found there was so much pressure, and a lot of it self-inflicted,' says the '93 champ. 'You put so much pressure on yourself to be the best that you've got to keep telling yourself that it's fun, because if it ever quits being fun it's really not worth it, because however much you're making, there's a lot on the line, you could get hurt in nothing flat. When I wasn't liking it anymore, I decided to stop. The thing with Rossi is that he's having fun, so he's out on the track every time wringing the bike's neck, trying to get everything he can out of it.'

Fellow American Roberts, who went on to become a successful team owner after winning his three 500 titles, agrees with Schwantz. 'I think Rossi's secret is pretty simple,' he says. 'It looks to me like he's loving it, he's happy to be out there. He doesn't play mind games, he loves riding the motorcycle, and he rides it right. That's a hard combination to beat; then when you get the best rider on the best bike, that's a hard combination to beat, too. If he keeps going like this, he'll set a lot of records and be one of the best, for sure. He's is definitely up there, but only time will tell if he's the greatest ever. The only thing that could happen is that he'll get burned out, but I don't see that, he's having more fun than anyone else.'

And yet, is this impression of a straightforward young man having a ball the real Valentino? Maybe not entirely, believes Giampiero Sacchi, the urbane Italian manager who brought the mop-haired 16-year-old into GP racing back in 1996. 'The Valentino concept is this,' says Sacchi. 'He wants other people to think that he's just having fun but for sure he's not just having fun, inside he's saying: "You think I'm just crazy but I'm not". I think this is the key to understanding Valentino; you watch him and it looks like he's just having fun, but if you watch him more carefully you realise there's nothing casual about what he does, everything happens for a reason, his is a very studied performance, he's thinking about all the details, all the time.' In other words, there's a fair dose of cunning in his make-up. Of course there is, no guileless rider ever won a World Championship.

No wimp ever won a World Championship either, so how come someone so apparently sweet-natured as Valentino has carved such a swathe through the sport? Bike racing is a vicious game, and while he isn't the kind of rider who strikes fear into rivals by riding out of control, there's no doubt that he takes no shit from anyone when he's on the racetrack. Scary aggression, intimidation and a bit of argy-bargy are all part of racing. 'GP riders don't mind riding into each other,' says Jeremy McWilliams, a stubborn rival during Valentino's ride to his first 500 win at the 2000 British GP. 'You want to pass as cleanly as possible, but if you're getting frustrated and it's the last lap, you ride into the guy. And it helps if you've got a bit of a reputation for being crazy. You need to stamp your authority on the other guys when you're making a move.'

People love Valentino because he's capable of racing hard, working hard and enjoying himself. His rivals also work hard but most of them have forgotten how to get their kicks out of what they're doing. Work hard, play hard isn't a new concept but it's a concept lost on many of today's richly rewarded sports stars, whether they're Formula One drivers, tennis players or bike racers. And there's something deeply unattractive about watching someone getting paid serious money for doing what they love and yet remaining so determinedly miserable. Vale could never do that, whatever the hours he puts into his racing. 'And he really does work at it, more than I ever did,' agrees Doohan. 'He's in the garage till all hours of the night, going through stuff with the crew.' Which might go some way to explaining why he's so bad at getting up in the mornings. During his first year in 500s, Valentino badly overslept at the Catalan GP, missing half of morning practice. 'When I wake up I always have a big confusion for the first five minutes,' he says in mitigation. 'Then I remember: "Oh fack, I'm at world grand prix!".'

Few club racers are that laidback and his horizontal demeanour once again contrasts vividly with Doohan, who, you just know, would've been a very different person on race mornings, awakening like some psycho out of a dodgy Hollywood thriller, lying rigid on his back, eyes twitching from tight shut to wild stare in, well, the blink of an eye.

Burgess remembers the Catalunya incident. 'He arrived in the pits in a state of shock, he'd never missed a practice session in his life. When he was at Aprilia his chief mechanic always went down to his motorhome and woke him up, so now it's me that goes and knocks on the door.'

Burgess has always known how to extract the best from his riders. Before Valentino and Doohan, the Aussie helped Freddie Spencer and Wayne Gardner to world titles during the Eighties. He expects 100 per cent commitment both on and off the track, and when he doesn't get it, he tells them exactly what he thinks. Some other crew chiefs won't do that, they're too wary of destabilising their riders. There's no doubt that the Burgess tough love has played its part in Valentino's recent successes, and yet Burgess is clever enough to realise that his rider wouldn't react well to regimentation. 'Valentino is Valentino, and if you kill that off you may kill off the goose that lays the golden egg,' he says. 'You've got to let him be himself, he certainly doesn't clown around in testing and he's always well applied in practice. In that way he's like Mick, you never see him just riding around, he's on it every lap. He does his own thing after races, but I don't think that affects him, he's just enjoying himself.'

Valentino's character still shines through when he's getting messy at a Sunday night victory party. At Rio 2001, where he wrapped up the last-ever 500 title, he was the star attraction at a Honda celebration party. Sharing a table with mate Marco Melandri, Valentino refused to hog the limelight, instead turning it on Honda's even-younger guns – the Spanish

Telefonica Junior team of teen heroes Toni Elias, Juan Olive and Daniel Pedrosa, who went on to emulate Rossi's success in both 125 and 250 World Championships. He invited them to his table to give them a first lesson in heavy drinking, perching uncomfortably on the corner of his chair while Elias enjoyed the comfy part of the seat. That's not normal behaviour for a World Champion – most racers are takers, not givers. They say that nice guys don't win World Championships but Vale does seem to be an exception. He's a giver not a taker, which is why he takes the trouble to entertain his fans. Cynics may say that's all guile to raise his profile, and sure there's guile in there, but most of all it's youthful *joie de vivre*; boys just wanna have fun ...

Chapter 2

MAKING VALENTINO

Tavullia is your typical sleepy little Italian town, the dusty tranquillity rent asunder by an ancient Vespa struggling up the hill, its gnarled owner hunched over the cockpit, fag hanging from his mouth as he's swamped by a gang of grinning scooter kids, all knees, elbows and dodgy riding styles.

The town is perched on the spur of a hill a few miles inland from the Adriatic and is reached by the kind of twisting country lanes that can give youngsters a taste for speed, the lanes down which cops used to chase Rossi and his gang of grinning scooter kids.

Like most of Italy the place is steeped in history. Tavullia's hillside location made it an important vantage point during the conflicts that raged throughout the peninsula in the centuries that preceded Italian unification in 1871. Strongly socialist for the last century, the region was fiercely anti-fascist during the Mussolini years and a hive of anti-Nazi resistance during the Second World War. German occupation ended in September 1944 after a particularly bloody battle as the Allies pushed their way north through the area's Gothic Line defences.

Almost 60 years after the Germans were defeated Tavullia is firmly in the hands of an army of Valentino Rossi fans. One of the larger buildings in the town's little piazza is painted vivid yellow in celebration of the hometown hero, yellow number 46 flags flutter from house balconies, shop windows are crammed with Rossi posters and locals wander past wearing bright yellow shoes and bright yellow jackets.

Half a mile away, overlooking Tavullia from another hillside, is the house where Valentino grew up and rode a motorcycle for the first time. Dad still lives there, with second wife Lorena and their eight-year-old daughter Clara. A rusting Lambretta lies on its side in one corner of the garden, but there are few other signs that this is the home of Italy's greatest motorcycling family.

Graziano Rossi wasn't as fast as his son, but he was one of Italy's quickest in the late Seventies and probably would've gone on to win more than just three GPs if his career hadn't been blighted by a couple of serious concussions. You can't know Valentino without knowing his father; meet Graziano and you fully understand why Valentino is the man he is: warmer, smarter and more modest than your average racetrack maniac. Graziano is a bit of a hippy too, a bit of an eccentric, renowned for his wacky helmet designs, extravagant clothing and the apparently bizarre habit of sleeping in the back of his BMW estate when he's at the races. 'I'm really proud to have found the alternative way to live at GPs,' he smiles. 'I don't want to drive a motorhome, I don't want to stay in a hotel because the best time to be with Valentino is in the evenings, and I can't stay in his motorhome because he never goes to sleep before one. Anyway, I've set up the car nicely, with a mattress like my own at home. I know people point at me but I don't care, so long as Valentino doesn't say: "Stop, you're embarrassing me."' You've got to admit it, the guy's got a point.

Papa Rossi was born on 14 March 1954 to a cabinet maker and housewife based in nearby Pesaro, home to the Benelli factory and many Italian racetrack champions. 'Pesaro is Italy's capital of motorcycling,' he reckons. 'All the kids are into bikes, not like the rest of Italy where they're into soccer.' Mama Stefania was born three year later, the daughter of a nurse and a bike-mad truck driver. They were neighbours as kids and got together when they were teenagers, by which time Graziano had already discovered his love of speed while racing his mates on pushbikes. 'We'd have races on the way home from school and I was the fastest downhill,' so it was only a matter of time before he was scraping around for an engine.

'We had no money but my best friend Valentino was a genius with his hands, he got an engine from here and a chassis from there and built our first motocross bike.' Rossi had wanted to go roadracing but his parents wouldn't sign for his licence, so he started on the dirt. 'For me roadracing was always the dream, it was more colourful, more important and all the real heroes were roadracers, anyone could do motocross.'

The pair worked in seaside restaurants and hotels to scrape together cash for their homebuilt racer until one summer Valentino was drowned in the Adriatic. Graziano still sheds a tear at the memory. 'Many people think we christened Valentino because he was born two days after St Valentine's day, but he's named after my best friend. He'd be Valentino even if he'd been born in December.'

Rossi started roadracing when he was 21 and quickly established himself, graduating to GPs within a few seasons. He enjoyed his greatest year in 1979, winning his first GP in the former Yugoslavia, four months after Valentino was born. Stefania gave birth on 16 February in Urbino, a few miles further into the hills from Tavullia. Urbino was also birthplace of Rafael, one of the greatest painters of all time, and the walled Renaissance city has remained largely unchanged in half a millennium.

Graziano and Stefania had been married in October 1978 when Graziano was recovering from one of his crashes. The couple divorced in 1990. 'I think he only married me because he was confused!' smiles Stefania, who's now in another relationship and has a second son, Luca. 'We met at such a young age, I think that's why it didn't work.'

Rossi won another two 250 GPs in '79 for the local Morbidelli factory and was then snatched up by Suzuki to contest the following year's 500 World Championship. But a nasty rally car accident left him nursing head injuries and his career lost momentum. Nevertheless he managed to get a ride with Giacomo Agostini's Marlboro Yamaha team in 1982, which ended with a horrific 150mph crash at Imola. His career was over. 'I finish racing because I almost finish to be alive,' Graziano laughs at the dark moment, which renowned GP medic Dr Claudio Costa eased him through. 'I was in coma for half day, I was Dr Costa's first miracle!'

Three-times 500 champ King Kenny Roberts remembers Rossi fondly, as a bit of a crasher. 'I recall one time he was scaring the shit out of me, and, of course, he ended up in a heap. I always knew that about him: "Okay it's Rossi, make sure you're not right on his ass coming out of this turn," you needed an exit plan, so I always gave him room.'

So Graziano was scary, but with a great mind and a heart of gold, according to former racing correspondent Barry Coleman. 'He rode like the wind and was a literary man, so we'd sit in his awning and discuss writers like Alberto Moravia (a 20th century Italian novelist). He'd say interesting things, like he'd wonder if racing was humane. He told me that whenever he saw someone crash he had a huge temptation to stop and help, which he had to repress; that's just too peculiar for a racer.'

Even if Valentino has no more than the haziest memory of his father's career, he now knows all about what Graziano got up to on the racetrack. When I told him about my own youthful regard for his dad, Valentino wanted to know why I was a fan. I said I liked the way Graziano could lead a GP by several seconds, then crash on the last lap. 'Yes, yes!' he replied, his face brightening in instant recognition. 'That's my father!'. On balance Valentino has done well out of his dad, inheriting some good genes and benefiting from an upbringing rich in paternal warmth, intelligence and riding tuition.

Valentino had his first ride on a motorcycle when he was two and a bit. Neither father nor son remember what the bike was, but it came with outrigger safety wheels which lasted just three days. Surprise, surprise, he seemed to have a natural gift for it. 'He was pretty instinctive from the start,' says Graziano, who worked as a primary school teacher before his racing career took off. 'I was surprised by how little I had to explain, but I now think that kids of that age have more ability than we ever imagine.'

Stefania wasn't exactly thrilled to see Valentino getting into bikes but she too realised he was a natural. 'I could see that he wasn't dangerous, just from the way he was, the way he rode and I wasn't too protective as a mother,' she says. 'I was a lot more worried when Graziano raced! He made me too nervous, so I didn't go to many races.'

But Valentino did go to enough races to absorb the thrill of speed, colour and noise. Graziano remembers: 'After I retired I was friends with riders like (Loris) Reggiani and (Luca) Cadalora, so we'd go to grands prix to watch them. Valentino's first memories are of the paddock and when he was at home he played with motorbikes instead of other toys, this was just natural, he was never pushed. Around the age of four or five he was very curious and was surrounded by some great riders, so he'd always ask 2,000 questions to everyone, as any kid would do. People would disappear if they saw him coming, he was a pain in the ass at those times, but in general he was a bright and lovely kid.'

And pretty soon Valentino was trying to emulate his heroes. 'I remember my first big crash. It was '84 and I'd seen Randy Mamola hanging so far off his Honda 500 that his outside foot was off the footpeg. I went home and tried to do the same with my BMX bike and had a highside. Fack, I had a huge bruise and very much pain in the ass.'

So he was already getting a kick out of risk taking. Most kids take risks somehow, it's one way of finding out what they can get away with and how they relate to the world. One child might slap the face of a playmate, another might climb a tree, Rossi did daft things on bikes.

If mum wasn't much worried about their boy getting into motorcycles, Graziano was concerned. So he built him a go-kart, and not just any old go-kart. The chassis had been designed to take a 60cc grass-cutter motor and a ten-year-old driver, so Graziano bolted in a 100cc national kart motor and gave it to his five-year-old son. It was, dad remembers, 'an evil thing', and so fast that no one could stay with Valentino during their outings to local gravel pits. Here the gravel-pit gang – Rossi, Reggiani, Cadalora & Co. – would race around in beat-up rally cars, just for kicks. 'We had old Ford Escorts and Opel Asconas. We'd race around the pits and Vale was always faster in his kart. The ground was great for learning, not so much grip so he'd be sideways all the time.'

Both Rossis have a passion for rallying and the gravel-pit gang still hang together today. 'We still go very often,' says dad. 'Me, Aldo (Drudi, racing's favourite graphic designer and the man behind both Rossis' helmet designs), Uccio (Vale's childhood mate and constant companion) and others, it's a nice way for friends to get together. Valentino is the only pro there and it's a big pleasure for us to watch him drive and do things. He grew up amongst racers, so it's always been with him, but there was no future seen in any of this, it was just fun, though maybe a bit dangerous.' Dangerous, for sure, but the kind of distraction that can stop kids growing up to be crackheads.

Meanwhile Valentino was getting on with primary school in Tavullia. Mum wanted him to grow up to be an engineer but while he was bright, he wasn't the most dedicated of pupils. 'He didn't used to feel like studying,' she remembers. 'But he had a great memory, so I'd read his school books to him while he lay on the couch and he'd get what he needed from that. He was a good kid, the kind that would get all the other kids together, his teachers always talked about that.'

If bikes and cars were the core of his childhood world, Valentino also showed a talent for guitar and football, although mother's efforts to take him to soccer school failed to distract him from his need for speed. And when his dad wasn't taking him to the gravel pits or to another GP, Vale would be sat in front of the TV, entranced by the great racers of the day. 'In F1 my heroes were Senna, Prost and Mansell, in bikes, Kevin Schwantz, Doriano Romboni and Loris Capirossi. Always Schwantz because he was the most spectacular and most beautiful on the bike, and also because of the colours. The style has always been important to me, and he was riding the Pepsi Suzuki then.' Even today the best compliment you can pay Valentino is to tell him that he rides like Schwantz. They both have an element of the cavalier in their riding and they've both got long, gangly, sticky-out legs.

Inevitably, the day came when Valentino wanted to go racing. He was nine at the time, a year too young for his junior kart licence but that wasn't going to stop the family from getting started. Remembering his own parents' refusal to sign for his racing licence, Graziano forged some documents with inside help from Tavullia's townhall, but their efforts were thwarted by a silly mistake. So Valentino had to wait.

Valentino was fast from the day of his very first race in early 1989, what a surprise. In 1990 he won the regional championship, enjoying his first victory that April, but by then he'd already spotted the toy he really, really wanted. 'The end of '89 was the start of the minimoto craze, there'd been nothing like minimoto before,' he says. 'As soon as I saw these bikes I wanted one, so I pushed and pushed my father until he bought me one. It was black, like Ron Haslam's Elf Honda GP bike.'

Right away it was obvious that this was what the boy really enjoyed: riding round and round in circles, grinding his kneesliders to dust, just like the big boys. And he wasn't the only one. It seemed like all the local kids had these Lilliputian racers which they'd thrash around the mini racetracks that pockmark the nearby seaside resorts of Rimini, Riccione and Cattolica. Not just the kids either, anyone could rent a minimoto for a few thousand lira any day of the week and pretty much any time of day or night. Teenagers would come tumbling out of the local nightclubs, well the worse for wear, and end up in a heap in the middle of some tiny racetrack, giggling until they puked. 'The whole area went crazy on minimoto, we used to ride them around tracks made for radio-controlled cars. At first it was four of us, then six, then 35, just riding around for fun, not proper racing.'

Vale wasn't the fastest of his gang, at least until the racing started for real. 'It was at Miramare in the summer of '91 and it must've been one of the first proper minimoto races. I remember it very well, the great atmosphere and the floodlights, because it was night. We used to ride at Cattolica on Wednesday evenings, then go to Miramare. There'd be so many people there, like a World Championship, because there were all the rent-a-racers too. There were 20 in the race and I was able to go away out front, it was a surprise because I'd never been fastest before.' Vale won another 15 races that summer, invariably running number 46, the number his dad had used to win his first GP in '79, and wearing a Schwantz-replica Arai with a glued-on Ninja Turtle along for the ride. The childhood Ninja Turtle fetish is still there – one of the creatures standing guard in his motorhome as he gets dressed before riding.

It's impossible to overestimate minimoto's crucial influence on the career of Rossi and his peers. 'You think of any Italian racer my age or a bit younger – Melandri, Poggiali, Sabbatani, Brannetti – they all came from minimoto. The first time I went to the track at Cattolica in December '89, Melandri was already there, he was only seven at the time but he was already a phenomenon.' Of course, Marco Melandri went on to succeed Rossi at Aprilia in 2000, winning the 250 title two years later, Manuel Poggiali won the 125 world title in 2001 and both Max Sabbatani and Alessandro Brannetti got GP rides. 'Minimoto helped me very much. There would usually be four or five guys racing together, bumping into each other, so it taught me how to be aggressive, how to fight with other riders and how to overtake. Sometimes we raced in town squares, around tracks marked out by straw bales, so you'd have to learn to control the bike on bumps and slippery tarmac. It was difficult to overtake at some tracks, but I never had a problem.' He was already summoning up those weird lines that no one else even considered, showing the skills that would help him conquer the world.

And yet however hard he raced as a kid, Valentino's personality always shone through. He was already forging the characteristics that would serve him so well in adulthood and his mother soon recognised that he had a special attitude, unlike most kiddy racers who'd sulk or bawl whenever they got beaten. 'I was always impressed by how he always had fun with the whole thing,' says Stefania. 'He was really passionate about paddock life, he'd talk about that, or about battling with another rider, for days. He'd win one race, then maybe lose another or crash, but he liked the whole thing, not just the winning.'

Stefania reckons Valentino hasn't changed in that respect. 'It's his easygoing attitude, it's not something he was taught. The things I really like about him are the personal stuff. If I had to tell you what's his best quality, it wouldn't be his riding talent.' But then she's his mum, she would say that. And yet talking to Stefania and Graziano it's obvious that both have an extra-special love for their son, there's huge warmth within this family unit, even if the parents split over a decade ago.

Following the divorce Vale moved in with his mum. 'Living with her was very much easier,' he recalls. 'My father always gave me a hard time if I came in late or something, but my mother never did that, she was much calmer. We were all happy though, because they still had a good relationship and lived near each other.'

Nonetheless Giampiero Sacchi, the man who gave Rossi his first GP ride in '96, believes the split may have had some kind of an effect on the youngster, albeit ultimately beneficial. He names two other recent champions to support his argument: Max Biaggi, whose parents split when he was very young, and Doohan, whose dad died when Mick was 11. Divorce can shatter lives but childhood troubles can strengthen some characters, giving them an inner strength, a spirit of independence. 'I've come to the conclusion that to be so strong in your life you probably need to have been in some difficult corners,' says Sacchi. 'I understood that when Valentino was doing 125s with me. These young guys are not living a normal life. A normal kid of 16 or 17 is okay thinking about school, he's not ready to think about racing 16 GPs, travelling all over the world and fighting for a World Championship. I don't know whether these guys are crazy or not, but sure they're special.'

Like Stefania, Graziano is also well aware of his son's special qualities. 'His approach to racing has always been the same. Even now when he has a bad time in qualifying or he doesn't win the race, I see the same face that I sometimes saw when he was a kid, the tears lurking. He gets so involved and cares so much, he always has done, but he doesn't take it home. I think karts were a good schooling because he quickly learned how to lose, while he's always found it easy to be fast on bikes.'

Graziano likes to think he taught his son nothing, not through teaching anyway. 'I'm sorry about that,' he laughs. 'But I never had the chance to teach him anything because I quickly understood that he didn't want to hear my suggestions. Later on it got worse, if I suggested something he'd do the opposite! In general, parents can't teach their kids anything through words, it's from the way that they behave that kids pick up things. But there are some things I see in Valentino which I hope do come from me and that's his ability to have fun, to take things easy and not to dramatise life too much. Also, he wants to give the fans more than just a good race, and I hope he took that from me too. What I've learned from Valentino is total straightforwardness and sincerity, even if these days those characteristics sometimes get him into awkward situations.'

Graziano sees one quality in his son which he knows he never had, and that's the champion's killer instinct. Any racer who thinks about pulling over when he sees someone crash obviously has a bit of a problem. To most racers, though they wouldn't admit it, a downed rider is just one less man to beat. It's a hard sport, people die and get crippled in motorcycle racing, and most riders have little room within themselves for sympathy or concern. It's a denial thing, if they opened up to others' suffering or the possibility of their own, they'd probably end up quitting. Sure, Valentino isn't your average racetrack psycho, he's a sweet and charming human being, but some kind of transformation obviously takes place within him when he's on the racetrack.

'There's one difference between myself and guys like Valentino, Doohan and Biaggi,' says Graziano. 'And that's the fact that I never won a World Championship! Valentino has this thing, the quality of a World Champion. When he shuts his visor and starts a race everybody becomes his worst enemy, he needs to fight these people and he needs to win. When I was racing I noticed that World Champions have this ability to shut off from the normal world. I didn't have that and that's why I don't have a World Championship.'

In dodgy psychological speak, Valentino has a Jekyll & Hyde character. No surprise there because there are plenty of nice guys racing motorcycles who are transmogrified the moment they ride down the pit lane. Until they return they are possessed, prepared to take the kind of risks, with their own lives and those of other people, which they'd never dream of taking in normal life (except, of course, when driving a rent-a-car). And yet these contrasting on-track and off-track characteristics aren't difficult to reconcile in Valentino's personality. It really is very simple: going fast is a gas and winning is a laugh, and while these actions require doing some pretty scary things, there's no requirement to bring the maniac with you when you climb off the bike. It's just that some racers get so wound up in it all that they forget that. 'If you win it's very much better,' grins Valentino. 'But I never say to myself: "Ah fack, arriving in front is all that matters", I'm not obsessed. But, especially over the last two or three years, I know that I can win if I stay relaxed and concentrated. Maybe other riders like Biaggi are more angry with the other riders. I'm not angry with the other riders.'

So whatever Graziano says, it's obvious that he has taught his kid plenty. 'For sure I sometimes did the opposite of what my father told me,' admits Valentino. 'That's normal between father and son. If I make a mistake it's necessary that it's my own mistake. But he told me a lot of things and I often followed his advice. Whenever someone gives me advice I quickly decide whether it's bullshit or not. If it's not bullshit, I follow it.'

At the end of '91 father and son had an important decision to make. Rossi was still racing karts at this stage, minimotos were just for fun. He had finished fifth in that year's national kart championship at Parma and was ready to graduate to the Italian and European 100cc series in '92; the next step in a career that might have taken him all the way to F1. 'My plan was still for Valentino to race four wheels because I was scared he'd get hurt on a bike,' says Graziano. 'But two things changed this. First, he really, really liked minimoto, he used to spend all his days riding. Second, we realised that karts were getting too expensive for us, and we knew that car racing is all about money. If you don't have the best kart or car, you don't have much chance.'

Valentino takes up the story. 'We'd arrived at this point where we'd need 100 million lira for the '92 kart season, so I said to my father, "Maybe it's better we race with the bike," and he say "Ah, bo, really?". I say "Yes, so is it possible we race bikes?". He say "Yes,".'

So throughout '92 Vale, concentrating exclusively on minimoto racing, continued to learn the essentials of riding a motorcycle on tarmac just as fast as it'll go. 'But I was still just playing, not really thinking about the future. I wanted to win just like I wanted to win in karts, I think that's normal for a boy.' And win he did, all the way into '93, growing more serious about his racing by the day and growing taller too. It became apparent that soon he'd need a real motorbike.

Chapter 3

KIDS THESE DAYS

Graziano Rossi's memory is a bit iffy at the best of times – blame a few too many bumps on the head – but he has a vivid recollection of his son's first race on a real motorcycle. And if all of dad's stories are scattered with laughter, this tale fills him with particular glee.

'We were at Maggione in spring of '93, practising for Valentino's first race on his Cagiva 125. He got on the bike, rode 100 metres out of the pit lane and crashed at the first corner. So he came back and we fixed the bike. An hour and a half later the bike was okay, so he rode down to the first corner, no problem, then second corner, crash!'

Graziano loves this story because, like most bike racers, he sees a harmless crash as something to laugh about, which makes two crashes so close together almost hilarious. Most of all though, he likes the story because of what happened right afterwards.

'When he got back to the pits we were thinking: "Are we doing the right thing here or are we making a big mistake putting him on a proper bike?" It wasn't so good. For sure, Valentino was also wondering if this was his job for the rest of his life, and there was an important look between us. We didn't exchange words but what I'd meant with that look was: "Yes, this can still be your job if you want, don't give up".' There he goes again, teaching without actually saying anything.

'You could see the disappointment in Valentino's eyes, he was almost crying. But these are the most important moments in a racer's career, when you find the strength to react and to show whether you're strong or you're weak.'

Valentino did indeed bounce back that weekend, finishing ninth in his first-ever race on a full-size bike. Later on the world would see him perform similar comebacks time and again, until they became a defining feature of his career. He did it in his first 125 World Championship season, recovering from a rash of crashes to win his first GP, he did it in his first and second 250 campaigns, putting tumbles and miserable results behind him to go on to dominate. And he did it again when he graduated to 500s, dismissing two confidence-sapping get-offs to quickly assume mastery of racing's most challenging category.

There's obviously a pattern here, both in the cock-ups and the comebacks. 'It's a system,' says Valentino, explaining the crashes. 'Whenever I ride another kind of bike the beginning isn't fantastic, I make mistakes. I try to ride fast, I make mistakes, I need this to go faster.' It makes perfect sense, really. In racing there's only one way of locating the absolute limit and that's by tripping right over it. Once you've crashed you've found it, the next trick is to remember where it is, and a lot of racers never quite manage that part of the process.

Possibly even more miraculous than his ability to lock on to the limit, to the extent that he can dance along it all day, like he's taking a walk in the park, is his ability to stay cool when things go bad. 'Yes,' he says. 'This is very important, this is the key.' Again, many riders don't have this facility. Once they've started digging a hole for themselves they keep digging. It's just too easy to fall into this trap because racing is all about confidence and focus, and big, scary crashes tend to destroy both, unravelling even the greatest of talents. Probably it is only the real greats who can recover from such situations, but who knows how they manage that, via a Zen-like inner state or sheer bloody mindedness? 'I don't know how,' offers Valentino. 'Just that I've had some difficult periods but so far I've arrived at all my targets.' His Honda engineer Jeremy

Burgess begs to differ: 'Determination is the thing that unites the champions, that and a real fear of getting beaten.'

So he was rightly delighted with his ninth place at Maggione, although he remembers that crunching first day of practice somewhat differently from his father, and this isn't the only time their memories conflict. 'Yes, I crashed at the first corner but next time I made three or four laps before I crash.' In mitigation he adds: 'It was early morning, very cold, and new tyres.'

The race was the first round of that year's 125 Italian Sport Production Championship, open to hotted-up 125 streetbikes like Valentino's Cagiva Mito. This wasn't the first man-sized bike he'd ridden though. The previous summer he'd sneaked out at Misano, riding a mate's Aprilia SP racer. 'I was still too young to go on a real racetrack, so it had to be secret. My friend signed on, then I wore his leathers. This was my first time on a proper motorcycle and a proper racetrack, it was like a dream.'

Valentino didn't set the world alight in 1993. He made more mistakes, of course, but by season's end he was quick enough to take pole position at the Misano finale and finish the race third behind Andrea Ballerini and Roberto Locatelli. Both these men moved into GPs before Rossi, Locatelli going on to capture the 2000 125 world title.

The following year was very different. Rossi had an official Mito, supplied by Cagiva team manager Claudio Lusuardi, with which he recorded his first national victory at Monza. By the Misano finale he only needed a third-place finish to claim the title. 'I was third into the last corner but Stefano Cruciani arrive much too fast and knock me wide because he's facking crazy. I finish fourth, then they disqualify him, so I am the champion.' Cruciani, by the way, never made it to GPs. During '94 Rossi also became acquainted with life on slicks, contesting the Italian 125 GP series aboard a Sandroni, an

Aprilia-engined special built by Pesaro engineer Guido Mancini, the engine provided by Aprilia race chief Carlo Pernat, an old mate of Graziano's.

So he was getting pretty busy with his racing, which didn't leave much time for school. If he wasn't playing truant to go riding, he was struggling just to get out of bed in the mornings, a habit that would stay with him into his first year of 500s when he famously slept through morning practice at the Catalan GP. His love of the lie-in compelled him to find a new way of getting to school and he hit on the idea of using the family's Ape car, a rather comical three-wheeled pick-up powered by a desperately overworked scooter motor. Stefania remembers: 'Getting the bus to secondary school meant he'd have to get up earlier, so he'd wake up at the last minute, grab the Ape and fly down the hill to Pesaro.' Soon all his friends had Apes. 'At first, everyone looked at me like I was an idiot but the Ape became our gang's official means of transport, we even used them to go to the disco!' Once again Valentino was showing a tendency to stand out from the crowd,

And of course, all this youthful exuberance got him into trouble with the local police. 'There was a time when Valentino, his friends and their scooters caused total panic around this area,' says Graziano, a proud dad's grin spreading across his face. Nothing serious, mind. 'They were always getting chased by the cops, and at one time it was like open war between them, they really hated each other. They got chased down a dirt road and the police car ended up in a ditch.' You can imagine the scene, straight out of a Keystone Cops movie: the cop car teetering on its side, steam rising from beneath the bonnet and the sweating Carabinieri in their bulging tunics and pompous hats, shaking fists and screaming obscenities. In fact, this is another case of father's and son's memories diverging. Valentino doesn't remember the incident, but even if this is Graziano's memory playing tricks on him again, it's too good a fantasy to remain untold. This is what Valentino remembers: 'We were racing along the road from Pesaro to Cattolica on our scooters, like we always did, and suddenly we arrived at this police road block. I tried to escape by diving down a dirt road and crashed. So I kept quiet and waited for the police to go away but they didn't, so eventually I came out with my hands up. The problem was that they were looking for people with drugs, so they wanted to know why I'd been so keen to get away.'

His father goes on: 'That kind of thing is pretty normal around here. The good thing was that Valentino's group of friends were very close, this was just a big adventure for them. Getting chased by the cops and getting tickets was a downside, but they looked after each other, made sure no one got into real trouble.' Vale didn't survive his scooter days totally unscathed, however. In the summer of '94 he grabbed a lift to the beach with a mate, a car pulled out in front of them, breaking his left ankle and mangling a couple of toes.

If his racetrack results didn't yet put him head and shoulders above his rivals, he'd done enough to further prick the interest of Aprilia, who were signing a certain Max Biaggi to their 250 GP team at the same time. Pernat had liked Vale from their first meeting. 'I like him,' he says from behind his rarely removed black-out shades, 'because he remind me of Kevin Schwantz.' Aprilia provided a standard RS125R for the 1995 Italian and European championships and it was during those six months that Valentino came of age as a roadracer. He dominated the Italian series from the outset and made his first forays abroad.

'I think '95 was the best-ever European series because the races were run at the GPs. It was good because the GP riders would practice, then we'd be on the same track a few hours later, so we could compare. I watched all the 125 GP sessions and races.' During his travels he struck up a friendship with

Japanese 125 GP rider Haruchika Aoki, who won the 1995 and '96 125 World Championships and then moved to 250s and 500s. 'I had always had a passion for Japanese riders because I was very much into graphics and colours. They seemed to come from another world, with crazy helmet designs and very different leathers. Both me and Haruchika used Diadora boots that year, that's how we got introduced, and every time we went to another track he would take me around for a lap and tell me important things. That was fantastic.' And this was the year that Valentino's first alter-ego was born. Rossi became Rossifumi, after wild-riding Japanese 500 star Norifumi Abe.

Aoki's teachings may have been vital but they took a while to sink in. Rossi spent much of his time abroad limping in and out of Dr Claudio Costa's Clinica Mobile, the travelling hospital that looks after GP racing's walking wounded. 'In the Euros I was always racing Lucio Cecchinello who had an HRC-kitted Honda which was impossible to beat. But I wanted to beat him, so I'd go, go, go, and after, crash, crash, crash.' Nevertheless he finished the series third, enough to guarantee him entry to the following year's 125 World Championship.

This time Rossi did a deal with Giampiero Sacchi, racetrack kingmaker, collector of old Gileras and a lyrical teller of racing tales. 'At that time I was Biaggi's manager and the idea came to me to make a team for the '96 World Championship,' says Sacchi, who later guided Manuel Poggiali to the 2001 125 title. 'I couldn't afford a big rider, so I came to an agreement with Valentino and his father. It was a good team with standard bikes but very enthusiastic and even then Valentino was Valentino. I'd never seen a rider who wanted to do things like fix all the stickers to his bike. He's always been very careful with the details, that was the first shock!'

Sacchi wasn't the only one in for a shock. First time Rossi shared a racetrack with his GP heroes was during pre-season tests at Jerez in southern Spain. 'Fack, it was incredible, they were so fast! It was like another sport, maybe four seconds a lap faster. I thought I would never be able to ride like that, I needed to learn another way to ride the bike.'

And learn he did. The '96 season started at Malaysia's old GP venue, Shah Alam, a tortuous track that winds its way through encroaching tropical jungle. Rossi finished a creditable sixth in his GP debut and followed that with reasonable enough rides to 11th in Indonesia and Japan, where the mates of 125 star Nobby Ueda thought he was a girl! Back on familiar ground at Jerez for the start of the Continental sector of the championship he was bang on the pace – on the front row for the first time and in the thick of a typically crazed ten-man battle for the lead. 'I was second out of the final corner but I crossed the line fourth, and exactly the same happened at the next race at Mugello. My bike was very slow, I had many good races that year, but also some big, crazy mistakes.'

Indeed, Rossi suffered more than 15 crashes during 1996. He was a young man in a hurry, too much of a hurry after missing the podium by a fraction in Spain and Italy. Desperate for his first pop at the post-race champagne, he crashed out of the next two races in France and Holland, although not before he'd secured his first GP lap record at Ricard. 'It was necessary for me to ride crazy because my bike was so slow, and when you ride like this all the time, it's possible you crash. At Assen it was damp, I started 20th and after three laps I was second, then crash. Crazy!'

That accident brought matters to a head within Sacchi's tightly budgeted little outfit. 'You can imagine that all these crashes weren't good for the team,' Sacchi recalls. 'Many came from Vale just not thinking; the tyres: cold! Give gas: crash! So we take him into the motorhome and I say: "Vale, how is it possible you crash so much?". But now I understand there are many riders who don't crash and who never make it. The lesson is this: if a young rider is very fast, he's going to crash. He needs to discover the limit, and without crashing it's impossible to find the limit.'

Rossi remembers that little chat in the motorhome like it was yesterday. 'I remember Sacchi's words, he say to me: "If you continue like this, the maximum possible is that you become like Kevin Schwantz [who had recently been forced into retirement by aching injuries], but if you want to become like Max Biaggi [then riding the crest of a wave in the 250 class], it's necessary you change." So I say to myself: "Fack, I continue like this!".' The Rossi/Biaggi agro may have been far in the future, but Valentino already knew he didn't like the 250 champ, Biaggi was too proud, too Roman for his liking. A few years ago you only needed to take a look at www.valentinorossi.com to guess what he thought of him: Biaggi's name never even appeared, just XXX XXXXX.

Despite all the tumbles, Valentino's speed hadn't gone unnoticed. Aprilia were impressed enough to give him some factory parts; a better cylinder and a carbon front disc brake, because he was shattering the standard steel discs. The trick gear made all the difference: third in Austria for his first podium, then his first pole position and win at Brno in the Czech Republic. Rossi had arrived.

At Brno he beat veteran 125 champ Jorge Martinez by a fraction after a frenzied final few laps. Martinez, like many of the older GP racers, greatly disapproved of the kamikaze tactics employed by these crazy minimoto-drilled kids. The Spaniard had started his long and illustrious World Championship career way back in '82 when racing was less frantic, if only because there weren't so many good bikes around back then. He even remembers seeing Graziano's toddler in the paddock, and ruefully remarked after his defeat: 'I should've taken my chance then and run him over'.

Sacchi, of course, had seen it all before. 'It's like a pack of wolves, a new leader arrives, pushes the limit and the old leader has to give way. When Valentino arrived at the front, Martinez said that his riding was dangerous, and people said the same thing when Poggiali arrived.' Martinez retired a year later.

Rossi should've won more races in 1996. 'But after Brno the bad luck came. I was leading at Imola when the facking sparkplug broke, then Tokudome took me out at the first turn at Barcelona. At Rio I had a bad crash in practice which gave me a problem with my shoulder, so I crashed again in the race. In Australia another 'plug break.'

All this was of little consequence, however, because Brno had rocked Rossi's world. Now he knew he was more than just part of the pack and that changed his whole perspective on racing. 'Until you win you don't know you can win.' Sounds obvious, doesn't it?. 'And the win made me more happy because I think maybe it's possible I can win some more.'

For '97 Rossi was afforded the full-factory treatment by Aprilia: a pair of expensively honed factory RS125Rs and a factory crew headed by Mauro Noccioli, Sacchi still fronting the effort. And it wasn't just the equipment and personnel that were better, Rossi was also new and improved, no longer a GP dreamer, now he knew he could win this thing.

'I had a very good bike for '97 so I knew in my heart that I could win. Winning the championship wasn't a surprise, though winning 11 races and not making too many mistakes was. Before '97 I always made mistakes – I had more than 20 crashes in '95, 15 in '96 and maybe only three in '97. I changed because when you understand your power you become more confident and with more engine you can be more relaxed. The better bike also helped my concentration because when you've got a slow bike you push too hard and sometimes lose concentration. And after you crash, crash,

crash you say to yourself: "Fack, it's better I don't crash" because the asphalt is very hard.'

Sacchi was well aware of the change that came over his young protégé that winter. 'His mind changed, he became another person, but maybe the biggest change happened when he won the first race in Malaysia, then he realised he could win all of them. He was now sure of himself inside, he had the conviction, something that normal riders don't have. For me '97 was a dream, like being in paradise.'

Rossi messed up only once all season, tumbling out of round two at Suzuka while planning a last-lap push for victory. 'I thought I could win, now I just think I'm an idiot,' he said after wandering back to pit lane, grinning all the way and waving to the crowd. Even when he was beaten he appeared unbeaten. On the few occasions he was defeated in '97 he giggled his way through the podium ceremony just like he'd won, so his Japanese rivals couldn't nurture a hatred of the guy that might help them push just a little harder. Nobby Ueda (who won the other four races), Tomomi Manako, Kazuto Sakata and Masaki Tokudome could do nothing but laugh with him. Maybe Vale wasn't conscious of what he was doing, but these days he seems more aware of the psychological benefits of grinning when he's not winning, denying Biaggi & Co. the pleasure of seeing him well and truly vanquished.

Ninety-seven was the year Rossi mania grabbed everyone, when he began the winning that allowed him to indulge his kink for dressing up and showing people a good time. He looked no less ridiculous out of his post-race fancy dress, his girly mop raging increasingly out of control as the season went on, especially when soaked in that stinking podium cocktail of warm champagne and sweaty leathers. At times the mane was kept vaguely in check by a girl's Alice band, and finally, after he'd secured the title, it was chopped off, the new and much tidier coiffure dyed blue with a blond number 1 at the back.

The fun and games began after he scored his third victory of the year at Mugello. If he was going to make the effort anywhere, he might as well do it there, where the Italian fans go to extraordinary lengths to get involved and make some noise. The most ardent of them bring along static, open-piped engines which are deployed on the hillsides surrounding the Tuscan track and then rev them to oblivion, joined now and again by bikers caning their own motors until they rat-a-tat-tat off their rev limiters. Fireworks, thunderflashes and hundreds of camp fires complement the megaphone madness to forge a war-zone ambience. 'Up on the hill it's another world, the crowd is coming crazy: drink, naked people on motocross bikes, it's crazy! I was up there in '96 when I wasn't so well known and blew up someone's CBR engine, ooops! In '97 I went up in the evening and it was very dangerous, everyone jumping on me, shouting "Rossi! Rossi!" There was this big wall of people and only one way out, through the shower block, so I rode my scooter through the shower block. If I hadn't, I'd probably still be up there now.'

So how was he going to entertain this bunch of crazies? In recent years it had become the fashion for winning riders to stop on the slowdown lap and find an obliging track-invading fan with the appropriate national flag. 'If I won I didn't want to do that, I wanted to ride around with something different.' So halfway through his victory lap he stopped by his fan club's encampment and rode on accompanied by a blow-up Claudia Schiffer. The doll had been in its wrapping for nine months: in case of victory, open box.

'Gibo and me bought the doll before Imola '96 but, fack, I didn't win there, so it stay in box until we win at Mugello. But the Claudia idea wasn't mine because this talk about the Biaggi thing with her hadn't happened when we got the doll, it was my fan club's idea to write Claudia Schiffer on the back!' The gag poked fun at Biaggi's rumoured liaison with Naomi

Campbell. The relationship between Italy's favourite two racers, such as it was, had deteriorated after Rossi had a go at Max on an Italian TV chat show, Biaggi fronting up to him in a Suzuka restaurant, saying: 'Stay quiet, I am number one.' Rossi's new profile had brought his feelings for Max into the open and the Italian media were in like Flynn. Asked by one shit-stirring journalist if he considered himself the Biaggi of the 125s, he cheekily replied: 'No, Biaggi is the Rossi of the 250s!' From now on the pair would be rival suitors for the affections of the Italian public, the opposing armies of fans colour coded for easy identification: Marlboro red for Biaggi, yellow for Valentino, his favourite colour.

Next time out in Austria Ueda cancelled the party, by four thousandths of a second, but normal service was resumed in France (minstrel's hat on the podium) and Holland (a carefully customised plastic Superman-style Rossifumi cape). At Imola, where he achieved his third straight win, he left it to his fans to indulge in some straightforward crowd anarchy – the hillside opposite the pits ablaze with yellow fan club T-shirts and giant cut-out letters proclaiming ROSSIFUMI COSMICO. From here on in, it was *Il fenomeno Rossi* all the way. Which meant, among other things, burgeoning interest from the ladies, as his mate Uccio remembers: 'We really enjoyed having so many girls around back then. Maybe some top riders or superstars worry "Is this girl coming to see me because I'm famous or does she really like me?", but Valentino didn't think like that, he always said "I don't care why she's coming to see me, I'm just happy that she is coming!".'

More wins followed in Germany (medieval torturer, swinging a mace), Britain (Robin Hood, brandishing a kid's bow and arrow), and Rio to make it six in a row. Late in August he wrapped up the title at Brno, three races still to go. He still counts that day the best of his many great days. 'Becoming World Champion is for sure the greatest moment and maybe the first one was best. That and the 500, because it was the 500.'

A month later in Indonesia, he won his 12th and last 125 GP, dancing on to the podium wearing a comedy head bandage. The previous weekend he'd been celebrating the championship in Tavullia and the night went all rock star on him: a few drinks, a couple of girls and a car crash. 'My popularity had gone from zero to huge, my life went from normal to not normal, so we made a big party with the fan club. Afterwards we went to a disco in Montecchio. We had two cars and there was a girl in one car and another girl in the other. For sure, whichever car I went in, the girl in the other car would be angry, so me, my father and Loris got into another car, a Porsche 928. On the way Graziano wanted to try the car, so we went to this industrial estate. I was in the back, on the phone, when Graziano started getting sideways, but he exited one corner too fast and it was a big crash. We took out a lamp post, I hit my head and had some problems in the night.'

The Italian papers went huge on the story. 'And they all wrote that I was driving the car. It was a big, big casino (Italian for row), fack, incredible!' This was Rossi's first experience of the dark side of the media and it shook him up. 'I was very, very angry, it was a big shock.' Until then he'd been more sociable with the media than any other rider, whiling away hours on Sunday evenings laughing and joking with journalists in circuit media centres. Maybe he'd been trying to get on the right side of the oh-so-fickle Italian press, although it really had looked like he was just having some fun. From now on, however, he'd be more suspicious of their intentions.

At the same time he was discovering another downside to fame – the impossibility of even walking down the street without getting jumped on. When he visited that autumn's Milan bike show the organisers armed him with a couple of security gorillas. 'But they pushed the fans around and I didn't like that.' So what to do for the big show at Bologna? 'I dressed up with dark shades, a wig like Ruud Gullit and a baseball cap. I looked just like another fan and didn't get hassled once all day.'

Of course, he only had himself to blame for being too much adored. So does he ever regret having played the showoff? 'Sometimes, but I think I give good fun to people, though most of all to myself. I love doing new things, like the nac nac (a precarious wheelie performed standing with only one foot on the 'pegs). In 2000 I make very much rolling burnout, in 2001 I make very much nac nac, it's always necessary to learn something new. Nowadays I'm still happy when I win, as happy as '97, but there's less time to organise things. Always the ideas are mine, except Robin Hood, that was Gibo. My favourite one? For sure the doll!'

The doll was funny, supremely silly but funny, and if some of the other gags were almost painfully contrived there seemed no harm in it. This was just an ingenuous teenager enjoying himself, determined to squeeze maximum fun out of every moment. And now that he'd squeezed maximum fun out of GP racing's kindergarten, he needed somewhere new to play ...

Chapter 4

DOING THE FUNKY CHICKEN

But was he really any good? The racetracks of the world are littered with the broken hopes of have-a-go 125 heroes who never quite developed their skills to meet the greater, nastier demands of 250 and 500 racing; demolished fairings, fractured bones, shattered careers. In 125s, being a psychopath is almost enough. If you're braver and madder than the other guys, you might just succeed, if only on those occasions when you don't end up in an agonised heap by the side of the track. Relatively speaking, talent and intelligence aren't essential to racing a puny 45 horsepower 125.

Valentino might not be any different. So far there'd been little indication that we might be witnessing the creation of an all-time great, because all he'd done was ride a 125 very well. But Aprilia were pretty sure they'd got hold of someone special, someone who would more than recompense them for the loss of the man who'd put the little Italian concern on the motorcycling map. Max Biaggi had quit Aprilia under a storm cloud at the end of 1996, defecting to Honda, whom he hoped would look after him when he was ready to graduate to 500s. The Roman did what was expected of him, wresting the 250 crown from his old employers and presenting it to Honda, who kept their part of the bargain, furnishing him with a brace of NSR500s for the 1998 season. So the much awaited Valentino v Biaggi showdown would have to wait a while longer …

Aprilia determined to nurture their new asset like a favoured son. They assigned Valentino one of their greatest pit-lane engineers, the squat, avuncular Rossano Brazzi, who had worked with Aprilia's original GP hero Loris Reggiani. Over the next two years Brazzi and Valentino would build a special relationship that continues today. 'We still have fun together,' Brazzi says. 'We meet up when he's back in Italy and go out for dinner. Most of these evenings end up the way they always used to, with the restaurant getting trashed.'

Brazzi was perfect for Vale: a dedicated technician but a warm and gentle human being, so unlike the cold-blooded, data-fixated brainboxes who populate some stretches of pit lane. And he knew exactly what he was dealing with from the word go. 'The quality of Valentino was evident from the first time I worked with him at Jerez at the end of '97,' recalls Brazzi. 'That was the first time he rode the 250 and he broke the lap record!'

So right away Valentino had proven that he was more than just a 125 nutter, and not just with his riding skill but also with his guile. He was only 18 at the time and yet he knew the eyes of the racing world would be upon him when he rolled up for his first ride. He therefore wanted to make sure he made a real impression, a psychological impact, so he got on to the Dunlop guys and asked them to bring some super-soft qualifying tyres. At the end of the tests he comfortably surpassed the 250 record. All of a sudden he was faster than mighty Max Biaggi.

Fortuitously, Valentino entered the 250 arena when Aprilia were at the height of their powers in the class. The RSW had long been the fastest 250 but that year it enjoyed a greater-than-ever advantage, because Honda's engineers had got their sums badly wrong with a brand-new NSR250. The '98 NSR was a dog, nothing more, nothing less. And not only did Aprilia enjoy superior speed, they'd also assembled their strongest-ever team, Valentino lining up alongside his childhood hero Loris Capirossi and the similarly experienced Tetsuya Harada. Harada had won the 250 world title at his first attempt in '93 and would almost certainly have been further decorated if he hadn't suffered some miserable luck. Capirossi had been the proto-Valentino, the first of GP racing's teen stars, when he won the 1990 125 crown at 17. The toothy, hard-riding Italian from Riolo Terme, an hour's drive from Valentino's hometown, had retained the title in '91 and graduated to 250s the following year.

Thus Vale seemed to be in an ideal situation: fast bikes and fast team-mates, so no pressure to succeed too soon. Not so. 'All the other bikes were shit but I had two foxes for team-mates, both with many years of 250 experience, and the atmosphere in Aprilia was terrible. All the chief mechanics were fighting, you know, it was an Italian team: "Ah you have the best cylinder", this and that and so on. For me it was difficult to ride like Loris and Harada because they have more experience, but I didn't want to arrive third behind them, because to arrive third was to arrive last.'

And yet there were reasons to be happy he'd made the move, rather than indulging himself by carrying the 125 number-one plate. 'Maybe the best thing about 250s was that I could get out of bed later! I had to get up at seven for 125 practice, and that was a big problem for me, in 250s I could stay in bed until nine.'

Comfy lie-ins notwithstanding, Valentino cites 1998 as the toughest and therefore most important year of his career. Just as it was Mick Doohan's injury-wracked '89 GP season that tempered the Aussie into an indomitable racetrack warrior, so it was '98 that helped make Valentino the man he is today, although his suffering wasn't so much physical as psychological. He was having trouble distinguishing his real mates from an ever-burgeoning gang of hangers-on and dealing with the deaths of two of his best friends in a car accident.

'It was the most difficult year for me, because everyone expected so much and I really felt the pressure. I was fast but

I made mistakes because I wasn't relaxed. I had some personal problems with some friends who weren't real friends. It was like a balloon, it got bigger and bigger, then it had to burst. There were too many people around who only stayed with me because I'm Valentino and I didn't understand this very quickly because it was something new. I needed some time to understand the situation and then I realised why I wasn't concentrating on racing. My level went down all year, until we hit the bottom at Brno.'

The racing started at Suzuka, where bike problems kept him out of the running. He was quickly realising that 250s were altogether tougher, requiring intricate set-up work. 'Unlike 125s, everything must be just perfect or you have no chance of getting on the podium, let alone winning. Also, I missed my friends in 125s, though in my first qualifying session I saw that there are just as many crazy guys in 250s!'

Valentino would find out just how crazy when the circus headed south for the Malaysian GP, staged for one year only at Johor, just across the border from Singapore. Wearing a new skinhead cut for the subtropical heat, he was right on it, qualifying on the front row for the first time and racing for the lead with Harada and Honda's Tohru Ukawa. Just a few corners to go and he was ahead but Harada stuffed it up the inside at the final turn, robbing the youngster of the grippy line and forcing him on to the dirtier tarmac. The crash was a big one. 'Maybe I should've let him pass but after leading I couldn't do that. As the Japanese say: "Necessary make win!".' The race wasn't the only thing he lost that weekend – a reckless bet with Capirossi cost him a further million lira. All his team-mate had to do was risk his life by jumping off a hotel walkway into the pool, a 12-metre drop with no run up.

On to Europe and another two crashes during Spanish GP practice suggested that Valentino was retracing his 125 GP learning curve – fast, furious and often floored. But Jerez also commenced a strong run of results, his first 250 points for a hard-ridden second behind Capirossi, and another vital lesson learned. 'I'd geared my bike for the fastest-possible lap; that's what I used to do in 125s because you could run the same speed all race. But that's not possible in 250s: the tyres slide very much, so you go slower through the corners, so your gearing ends up too high.'

Second again at Mugello and Paul Ricard, he arrived at hot 'n' dusty Jarama, outside Madrid, in mid-June, convinced he was ready to win. Once again he did lead, as he'd done at Johor, Mugello and Ricard, and once again he jumped off. If he thought the press would cut him some slack during his apprenticeship, he was very wrong. He'd made a few mistakes on track and now he would make his first off it: naively underestimating the fickleness of the media and his fans. 'Very many journalist, who I thought were my friends, said: "Rossi won very many 125 races but 250s aren't the same and he's made mistakes, he's stupid". This was really bad for me, but also really good because I found out who my real friends were. Before then I thought I had more friends than I actually did.'

He also copped plenty of flack for his post-race jinks at Mugello, where he stopped on the slowdown lap and changed into beach gear, riding back to the podium ceremony in flip-flops. 'People said bad things about that. It's like if you win every race of your career you're a genius, but if you finish second you're a facking clown!'

Despite the media casino, Valentino was having as much fun as ever between races; playing football and racing minimoto, motocross and radio-controlled cars with Melandri, who'd just started his first 125 GP season. His weakest point was motocross. 'So I'd ring Marco, tell him we don't need to ride today, then do a few hours riding in secret!'

The nights were just as hectic. 'The Saturday before Jarama we went to a crazy club in Riccione – a lot of people out of their minds, really high, it's incredible what the young do for enjoyment! And I nearly got into a fight. This guy asked me for a cigarette and I told him I don't smoke, so he asked me again, then he said: "You won't give me a cigarette because you're Rossi," he wanted a fight!'

There were other reasons he needed bigger muscles. 'I never did any proper training when I was riding 125s because the bikes are like bicycles. Then at the end of '97 everyone said I need to go to the gym to be stronger for the 250, but I don't go because I don't like. At Jarama it's very bumpy, I wasn't in control of the bike, that's when I understood I need more power. So my mentality changed, I started going to the gym and now it's one of my passions, if I don't go for some days I get frustrated. I think I'm in good shape now, with very much more power than two years ago.'

The weekend before the Dutch GP, the season's halfway point, Valentino and some of his real mates scootered six miles down the road to play the fan at the Misano World Superbike round. 'It was like being a kid again, we just laid in the grass by the side of the track, sunbathed and watched the racing.' And in the evening he joined Yamaha's larger-than-life Supers hero Noriyuki Haga for some serious drowning of sorrows. The Japanese had crashed out of both races that day and astonished Vale with his drinking ability.

Assen next and the big breakthrough. His hair dyed bright orange for the occasion, although unaware of the colour's significance to the Dutch crowd, he motored into the lead 'like I was in a plane' and won by 20 seconds. Capirossi and Harada both stopped with bike problems.

Brazzi was impressed: 'It took Valentino half a season to get used to the 250. The biggest problem that most riders face when they move up from 125s is that 250s move around more, they're more nervous, both on the power and in their general handling behaviour. Initially, that nervousness gave him some problems; he didn't like it when the bike started sliding around, but he soon understood that's the way it is, and after a while he realised that just because the bike is sliding doesn't mean he's going to crash. Then he understood how to use the sliding to his advantage, just as he did in 500s.'

His team-mates' Assen DNFs brought Valentino to within 19 points of series leader Harada, although he hardly dared believe he was ready to race for the title. Just as well, because he crashed again at Donington, caught out by a full tank of gas and hard race tyres. It was the end of a miserable weekend, Italy crashing out of the football World Cup on Friday night.

In Germany, two weeks later, he was a chastened third behind winner Harada and Jeremy McWilliams's privateer Honda. 'Maybe I could've made second on the last lap, but after Donington I had very much fear of crashing again.' The weekend at the tortuous new Sachsenring wasn't entirely wasted, however. 'I realised I was still having problems with slow corners on the 250. They're difficult because you need to go slow mid-corner, then lift the bike really quickly and give gas when you're on the fatter part of the rear tyre, like Doohan used to.' He was already laying the foundations for his drive to 500s.

But it only took a few weeks off to forget that hard-learned lesson. He spent the mid-season break largin' it in Tunisia with Reggiani, Melandri & Co. and returned to Brno rested and ready to race. This time he lasted just four corners before falling. 'It was possible I win but I made the mistake because the fight between me, Capirossi and Harada was too much.

Right: *Graziano's influence on his son has been immeasurable, all the way from riding bicycles.* (Rossi family archive)

Overleaf: *'When I grow up I'm going to be a bike racer.' Yes, course you are, Vale.* (Rossi archive)

Above: *'Go on my son!' Valentino has just finished third in the '93 Italian Sport Production series at Misano.* (Rossi archive)

Left: *And Ninja Turtle came too. Vale lays the foundations of his genius at a local minimoto track.* (Rossi archive)

Below: *The boy's a natural. Vale graduated to 125 streetbikes in '93, won the Italian Sport Production title in '94. The usual one year to learn, one year to win.* (Rossi archive)

Everyone say again: 'Rossi was okay with the best 125 but now he has same 250 as other guys, it's another story'. After Brno I took all the negative power and transformed it into positive power. I don't know how, I think I just understood better, so I became a lot calmer. It was a very bad time, but I arrived at the next races harder and more focused.'

Just four races remained in which he might prove to everyone that he was more than just a fast fool; two in Europe – Imola and Catalunya – and two outside – Australia and Argentina. Valentino won the lot, pushing Capirossi into second on each occasion. And he did so in style, wearing a tricolor hairdo at Imola and, still unable to resist playing the clown, riding his Catalunya victory lap with a chicken on the pillion. Well, a friend dressed up as a chicken. That jape got Valentino into conflict with series organisers Dorna, who were growing increasingly tired of the boy's displays, which might interfere with their precious race schedule and encourage fans to invade the racetrack. He was unrepentant: 'I'll do the same thing again because I like to amuse the fans. I think the GP bosses want to make motorcycle racing like F1 and I don't think that's right. I don't like F1 because it seems everyone is only there for the money, while bikes are about passion.'

The final win at Buenos Aires was achieved in blissful ignorance of a title-deciding contretemps between Capirossi and Harada. Harada had been running second at the last-but-one turn, good enough for the title, when Capi arrived at warp-factor five, wiping out the Japanese rider to claim the crown for himself. That left Valentino just shy of winning the

Previous spread: *Can't live with 'em; can't live without 'em. Rossi has attracted a whole new breed of fan to GPs, even if he doesn't have a big love for the Valenteenyboppers.* (Milagro)

Left: *Receiving useful advice from mate and double 125 World Champ Haruchika Aoki: 'Necessary cut hair'.* (Gold & Goose)

championship, too close for comfort: 'I lose the title by just three points, shit!'

Looking back at his first 250 season, he had done a lot of growing up, he was no longer the naive teenager merely out for some fun. 'That summer changed me in life and as a rider, it was a bad period but maybe necessary. I very much change my comportment in the paddock, when I am with people who are not my friends. I become more clever and less impulsive, so when I speak with journalists I stay more quiet, because it's like the police: "What you say may be used against you". But when I am Valentino, in my mind and with my friends, I maybe became less serious, maybe have more fun, because it's very necessary.'

During 1998 racing also ceased to be playtime and his 250 rivals weren't playmates. 'In 125s everyone is like a family, everyone stays friends, it's not like that in 250s,' he said halfway through the year. 'I don't like the way some 250 riders behave. Before I came into 250s a lot of them were my heroes, but not any more. Some guys like Ukawa get in my way and try and slow me down when I'm on a fast qualifying lap. Then they say they didn't see me, but for sure they did, no one ever did that when I was in 125s.'

No worries; he'd teach them. He knew he didn't need to change much for 1999, just his alter ego: out with Rossifumi, in with Valentinik. 'We needed a superhero to come back from the bad situation of '98. We were preparing to win in '99, so we chose a superhero based on Italian comic hero Paparinik. Paparino is Donald Duck in Italian and Walt Disney has a duck superhero called Paparinik, who wears a mask and a cape, but he's not like Superman, he's a little bit unlucky, he makes some mistakes, some casino, but at the end of every story he's always the superhero. Paparino becomes a superhero and becomes Paparinik, so Valentino became a superhero and became Valentinik!' Simple, really ...

And the 1999 world title could hardly have looked easier. Vale was now solo numero uno at Aprilia, Harada having graduated to the factory's 500 twin, Capirossi back at Honda after getting the flick for his Buenos Aires indiscretion. But if HRC had squeezed more speed from their NSR, the bike was still slower than the Aprilia, although marginally faster than the sluggish but sweet-handling YZRs of Yamaha's new challengers Olivier Jacque and Shinya Nakano.

The 16-race campaign began true to the Valentinik script: bike trouble at Malaysia's new space-age venue Sepang and a dismal seventh in pouring rain at Honda's grim new Motegi circuit; 'I still don't like riding under the water,' he explained.

Back to Europe, already a worrying 21 points down on joint series leaders Capirossi and Nakano. Time for another miracle renaissance. 'But this was different from '98, I was in a deeper hole in '98, this time I arrive at Jerez relaxed and, no problem, I win.' He coolly defeated Ukawa's NSR, Nakano retiring with bike trouble, and celebrated in hilarious fashion, dumping his RSW on its side and diving into a trackside Portaloo.

'On the Thursday I was jogging around the track with Uccio and we saw this toilet. I thought: "Why they have just one toilet out here, all alone?" So I say: "For sure, if I win I go in."' When he reappeared, the crowd went berserk.

Two weeks later it was Valentino's turn to suffer bike trouble. Cruising to an easy win at Ricard his Aprilia's drive chain jumped the sprockets, leaving him languishing trackside and fourth on points, 40 down on race winner Ukawa. Now there was a mountain to climb. 'I found myself in a strange situation. I was fighting for the title with Ukawa and though I knew I was faster, I knew I couldn't afford one mistake because the gap would increase to 60 points and I'd be facked. I always knew in my mind that I could beat Ukawa, but if he kept finishing second it'd take eight races just to catch him. So I stay quiet and relaxed.'

From here on in, he rode the knife edge like a master. He won eight of the last 12 races, finished second twice and third once, only missing the podium at rainy Valencia, still struggling with that water stuff. Poor Ukawa didn't know what had hit him.

The rout had begun on home tarmac at Mugello, Valentino's special home-race leathers and bodywork resplendent in swirly Seventies-style graphics, proclaiming 'Valentinipeace&love'. Aprilia Germany's Ralf Waldmann came in second at a respectful distance, Ukawa third. The race had been a walk in the park, the victory lap less so. Valentino ended up submerged beneath an ecstatic Latin throng killing him with their kindness. 'I was trying to escape the crowd, then I run into a cameraman and fall down. The Italians went crazy, it was a nightmare, I think I would die.'

Two weeks later at Catalunya, another win and fastest lap, Ukawa yapping at his heels all the way, but well covered at every turn. The next Saturday at Assen he looked very ragged, very unRossi, as Capirossi wreaked revenge, beating him by a fraction, with Ukawa, Nakano and Briton Jeremy McWilliams right in there too. 'Assen wasn't a race, it was a battle. That sometimes happens, you stop with the right lines and just fight, like remove one chip from your brain and put in another. It was me against Capirossi, and, fack, I lost.'

At least he'd got something of a buzz in qualifying, bettering Biaggi's previously unbeaten 1995 pole record. 'The Aprilia mechanics who worked with Biaggi in '95 were working on Harada's 500 in '99, and they kept telling me I'd never beat that lap. After the final session I couldn't resist going into their pit and having a little laugh at them!' The achievement mattered all the more because Assen is considered GP racing's ultimate test of rider talent. 'It's like a horizontal rollercoaster,' said Valentino, already wondering what it might be like on a 500. 'No problem on a 125, a little problem on a

250 and maybe a very big problem on a 500. Watching the 500s there is scary, they're so fast and wobbling all over!'

During July he paid back Capirossi, beating him by a fraction at Donington and Sachsenring, and all of a sudden he was leading the championship. If anyone had previously doubted the depth and breadth of the boy's talent, there could be but one or two doubters left, and Honda certainly wasn't one of them. The world's biggest bike brand wanted in on the Rossi phenomenon, Honda Italy and Doohan initiating a scramble that gained momentum until there was a hint of the rampant about it. Honda weren't going to take no for an answer. Hell, there hadn't been a bike star like this – so talented, so saleable – in decades. At first he played hard to get: 'I'm in no hurry, I'm not obsessed with doing 500s, I have a good relationship with Aprilia and I see no reason to leave.'

There wasn't just one offer from Honda either, there were two, one from Honda Europe and one from Doohan, who was planning to create his own team after suffering career-ending injuries at Jerez in May 1999. At Brno, where he won again to secure the first of two 250 hat-tricks, he was still thinking Aprilia. And by Imola he was already getting sick of people quizzing him about his plans.

If these were confusing times for Valentino, they must've been an absolute whirl for his hairdresser. At Donington in July he'd gone a hair colour too far: green, which followed less criminal cranial outbursts of orange, grey, blue, blond, black/blond and red/green/blond. Presumably realising the error of his ways, he quickly had the greened locks shaved off and then had his skinhead neatly adapted for Imola to replicate Brazzi's naked pate. Brazzi was touched by this grinning gesture of respect: 'It was typical of Valentino's nature, his way of joking with his people, his way of showing his appreciation.' Didn't work though. Valentino succumbed to Capirossi's Honda once again, his over-stiff and unstable

Aprilia lacking traction out of the slower turns. Luck was on his side once again, however, because closest points-challenger Ukawa limped in 12th after a mid-race tumble.

The next day he was holed up in an Imola hotel room, holding the first of many secret meetings with HRC personnel. 'They wanted me to say yes or no immediately, but I said: "Sorry, I want to win 250 before I make decision". The hard thing for me was leaving Brazzi's team because they'd become like family to me. But I told Brazzi then, "If I win title, my work in 250 is finished".'

After an eighth-place finish at rainy Valencia the circus headed out of Europe for the last four races, Valentino pursued everywhere he went by Honda representatives and an ever-growing pack of spying Italian journalists, gathered here and there in conspiratorial huddles. At windswept Phillip Island he somehow managed to keep his head in the midst of the feeding frenzy, recovering from a bruising crash in qualifying to win a classic four-way battle with Jacque, Ukawa and Nakano. 'During practice we didn't have so much rear grip and eventually we realised it was a gearbox problem; the gearing was too tall so I wasn't able to transfer weight to the rear tyre when I was getting on the gas. My mechanics lowered the gearing on Saturday evening and that made the difference.'

While his crew toiled on his RSW he sneaked across the makeshift Phillip Island paddock – all Portakabins and corrugated sheds – to visit the HRC pit. Inside was Jeremy Burgess, Doohan's crew chief who'd been twiddling his thumbs ever since the Aussie's bone-crunching crash at Jerez. Burgess was the man who would be looking after Valentino if he did make the switch and this was their first meeting.

'It was like when I first met Mick way back in '88; the important thing was to listen and to understand what he would want from us if he were to join Honda,' recalls JB.

'Then I showed him over the NSR500 and he listened to everything, took it all on board, even though I wasn't doing a salesman deal on him because he wanted a Honda, he knew it was the bike to do the job in 500s. He was very quiet, which I always think is a great sign of intelligence. I pretty much said to him that if he got to the top of Honda's pyramid of riders, we'd do whatever he wanted to make things work.'

One close look at Honda's money-no-object NSR was enough to make up Valentino's mind. 'When I see the bike up close I say: "This is the bike, maybe is necessary we go to 500 grand prix".'

Directly from Melbourne to South Africa, for the first GP at the brand-new and only just completed Welkom venue outside a gold-mining town fallen on hard times. Once again, Valentino and his crew battled set-up problems. 'We always struggled at slippery, bumpy circuits because the Aprilia has such a stiff chassis', but he won anyway. By now there was a sense of the relentless about the racing; after a messy start he casually brushed aside all opposition to head home Nakano's easier-handling YZR. If things kept going like this he'd clinch the title at Rio in a fortnight.

The Italian media could barely contain themselves, their hysteria tweaked more by rumours that he was defecting to Honda than by his genius stroll to the title. He found the fuss hilarious: 'They make a big casino because I will be racing against Biaggi for the first time. For sure Biaggi will be difficult to beat, especially in my first year. He's one of the best 500 riders, but at the end of the day he's only another rider.' The papers could see exactly what was coming.

At Rio he came back from another sluggish getaway to hunt down Capirossi, Ukawa, and Jacque, then saunter past to take his ninth win and collect the crown. Not only that, he also became the youngest 250 World Champ, taking the record away from the late Mike Hailwood who'd been 21 when he won the title in 1961. Valentino had flown 20 members of his fan club to Brazil for the occasion and celebrated with a riotous party at a nearby yacht club, where he was tossed fully dressed into the swimming pool. That same evening he made another clandestine visit to a hotel room, where he met the men from HRC once again. 'I say to the Japanese: "Okay, we are ready".'

Aprilia still had a bigger pile of cash on the table, their deal reputedly worth £2.3 million, although he refuses to talk numbers. 'I always knew Honda would be less money but at that point in my career I never think about money because is necessary to concentrate on racing.' Although the fine details were thrashed out at a later date, Valentino was destined to be his own one-man team, outside of the Repsol Honda clique, which allowed him to run his own sponsors, his own livery and his own favourite colour. 'When I make this kind of decision I try to go the way that gives me the most freedom. So with Nastro Azzurro and my other sponsors I can make a yellow bike. Yellow is my colour, like 46 is my number.'

It was back to business the following Sunday for the season finale in Argentina, where an incorrect tyre choice left him third behind Jacque and Ukawa. Or maybe his mind had been on other things: his bosses at Aprilia had generously granted him an early release from his contract, so HRC had booked Jerez for his first 500 test just four weeks hence. Okay, he could ride a 250 but ...

Chapter 5

A POET IN MOTION

All the racetrack and a little bit more, that's always been Valentino's style. His signature is the flurry of dirt kicked up from trackside as he carves an extravagantly wide line in search of the fastest launch out of a corner. It's a perilous technique, especially on a viciously overpowered motorcycle like an NSR500. It's tempting fate, then giving fate the finger, and that's exactly why he likes doing it. Plus, of course, going that extra centimetre is a key element in his ability to magic the best out of a racetrack.

'I always like to go to the edge, because it give me a power. If I can exit a corner for ten laps every time one centimetre from the edge of the track, I feel everything is under control. I've always had a big passion for the line, for me the line is like a poem. My focus is always for my lines to be within the same centimetre every time for 20 laps. This feels good, because you can do one fast lap all with your heart, with the eyes shut, but it's not easy to ride 20 laps like that. Sometimes I crash because of my passion for the line. Uccio and Gibo say "Fack, stay 50 centimetres inside", but it's my passion.'

Sito Pons Corner, Jerez, December 1999. Valentino is riding out of the circuit's most important turn, a blind 85mph right-hander that crosses the brow of a hill, then plunges the rider down into the track's fastest straight. He is looking stiffer than usual, a little hesitant, nothing like he had looked 30 days earlier in South America where he'd been master of a 96hp motorcycle. Now, here he was a few weeks later, a 190 horse motorcycle very much his master. He's exiting the corner, the revs building fast, then too fast as the rear slick loses traction and smears sideways, driving the motorcycle off the tarmac and across the kerb where he fights a mother of a tankslapper. He stays on but it's hardly poetry in motion.

'Valentino looked a little awkward on the bike initially, I mean it's a big step,' says crew chief Jeremy Burgess who has vivid memories of that first test with Alex Criville's title-winning NSR. 'I wouldn't say he was awestruck, he gave the impression that he was pretty much prepared for anything, but he was feeling his way that first time, he knew he had some learning to do.'

If anyone was awestruck, it was Burgess and his ex-Doohan crew: Bernard Ansiau, Alex Briggs, Dickie Smart and Gary Coleman. After years of sweating in the pressure-cooker of Mick's pit box they could hardly believe the aura of calm in which they found themselves. Burgess: 'The guys were like: "Jesus, isn't he great?" and I was saying: "Yeah, I know, it's fantastic". We had to do a complete mind switch because we'd gone from working for the grandfather, and thinking like that, to getting on with the mentality of a 21-year-old. For me, approaching 50, that was very enlightening and part of it was getting some enjoyment out of the way Valentino sees life.'

Pretty soon the guys discovered that Valentino wasn't just fun to work with, he also had real intelligence, an enquiring and analytical mind that would allow him to quickly convince any doubters that he really is one of the all-time greats, not just a great 125 and 250 rider. After a predictably shaky start, while he attempted to locate the 500's limit, he swiftly rose up to conquer his NSR and then the entire 500 grid. The group of riders who had been elevated to the status of title fighters by Doohan's crunching exit from racing only enjoyed the briefest moment of glory before Valentino had them done and dusted. His 13 500 GP victories from the next two seasons exceed even Doohan's win rate; 40.6 per cent to 39.4 per cent.

After Jerez, Burgess's first job was to revise the NSR's riding position for its gangly new pilot, then get down to the task of adapting every facet of machine performance to suit his riding style. 'From the start Valentino was very open about any problems he was having with the 500,' he says. 'And when we made modifications he was very open about whether they were an improvement or not. We quickly learned that he's very good at working on set-up. When he comes into the pits he's like a computer. He gives you a list of six or eight things he wants looking at, like a download. He's more analytical than the rest of them. I think we have a lot to thank his parents for because they gave us a kid who can think logically and also Aprilia, who gave him the training so he can say what the problem is and whether we're making the bike better or worse. But back at the start we could see that he was looking forward more to the racing.'

There was much to learn before the season started, although things were looking pretty rosy. After all, he'd just joined the factory that had won every 500 riders' and manufacturers' title since 1994, so there was no doubt he'd got his hands on the best 500. No doubt, at least, until the 2000 season actually started, when it quickly became apparent that something had gone very, very wrong with the NSR. This was the year that Honda lost the riders' crown to Suzuki's Kenny Roberts and its manufacturers' title to Yamaha.

The reasons for the upheaval in factory fortunes were several. Suzuki and Yamaha were trying harder than ever, and their riders, especially Roberts and Marlboro Yamaha's Max Biaggi, were coming nicely to the boil. Also, Doohan was no longer around at HRC, which put Criville top of the pyramid. Without the Aussie's guiding light HRC were lost in the darkness, the engineers making the mistake of listening to a rider, well, listening to a rider who didn't really know what he wanted from his motorcycle.

'It's like Honda did with Wayne Gardner when he won the title in '87,' explains Burgess, who had guided the rodeo-riding Aussie to the 500 crown after working with triple world champ Freddie Spencer. 'They asked what Wayne wanted and he asked for more power. That's what Alex asked for too. More power is easy enough, so long as you can open the throttle, but the new engine was very different in terms of power delivery. Later on an HRC engineer told me that Mick wouldn't have done half a lap with the 2000 engine, so I asked the guy: "Why the hell would you make it then?", but it was what Alex wanted. Alex didn't have the experience, he'd always just followed along in Mick's slipstream, beating him from time to time when things went his way.'

Incredibly Valentino clocked the dodgy power delivery the very first time he rode the new NSR at Phillip Island in early 2000. It took HRC's more experienced men longer to realise they'd got a serious problem. 'All the power had been moved to the top, so there was nothing there when you were fully leaned over in the middle of the corner, so you'd give it some more throttle and there'd be too much power,' Burgess explains. 'He said it felt too neutral in the middle of the corners.' Which is exactly why Valentino crashed on that first outing.

No worries; by round one at Welkom he was well up to speed, qualifying just a tenth of a second off the front row. He also set the fastest lap of the race, moments before he crashed out, losing his NSR right in the middle of a turn, like it just rolled over and died. Aussie terrier of slide Garry McCoy won the race, Carlos Checa second on a Yamaha, and Loris Capirossi third on a '99 NSR. Same deal at round two; Valentino low-level flying into a heap again, this time Roberts the winner ahead of Checa and McCoy. The factory Hondas were nowhere once more and within HRC the accusations began to fly.

Burgess could see from the computer readouts why Valentino was crashing and why the other NSR riders were struggling, but was unable to do much about it via HRC. 'Valentino was the new boy on the block, fourth in the pecking order behind the Repsol guys: Alex, Tady (Okada) and Sete (Gibernau). Plus he'd got no points on the board so we couldn't go in there screaming and shouting.'

Yet despite Valentino's deadly unimpressive start, HRC didn't take long to realise they had hired themselves an exceptional talent. While the media were already wondering if he'd got what it takes to cut it in 500s, HRC had some definitive evidence suggesting that he surely would. His data traces didn't only highlight the NSR's problems, they also showed that Valentino already had more refined throttle control, the essential weapon in a 500 rider's armoury, than other HRC riders like Criville, veteran of more than a hundred 500 starts.

HRC was also impressed with Valentino's fighting spirit. 'He was carving through the pack at Welkom and Sepang, trying to do what he thought he could do,' recalls Burgess. 'So they'd seen that he had the determination to get the bike to the front and this is what's very much rewarded at Honda. Anyone who just rides around doesn't get a lot of say, but there's always hope for the guy who pushes hard, even if he falls down, it's like: "We can work with this guy".'

Valentino didn't know that at the time and the two crashes had rattled his cage. He arrived at Suzuka for round three physically and psychologically bruised, and it showed on the track: 13th on the grid, 11th in the race, his worst result since his earliest 125 GP days. Perhaps this really was a class too far. 'Valentino was very, very badly spooked by the two non-finishes and he was very spooked by the 11th place. That Suzuka ride was a complete shutdown of a guy who could've done better.'

After Japan the circus returned to Europe. Would Valentino get it together on more familiar tarmac, or, having started digging himself a hole, would he continue to dig? The comeback at round four in Spain was as emphatic as those he'd managed in 125 and 250: first front-row 500 start and first podium behind Roberts and Checa. New engines parts, or rather old '99 parts, had arrived for Jerez and Valentino was back on a bike that he could work with.

'Once we got to Europe we started to kick off,' says Burgess who had quickly established an excellent working relationship with his new charge. 'You didn't have to be Einstein to work out what he was capable of. The talent was obviously there for anyone to see, so long as he was kept happy and kept in the right frame of mind. So I was emphatic with the team and everyone around us, I told them that this guy isn't going to fail unless we fail him and the only way we can fail him is if he's not happy within this team network. So the number one priority is to keep him happy.'

Racing is all in the mind, so Burgess's job is to ooze confidence, to instill his rider with the belief that he really can go that extra two tenths faster. 'In this game it's 80 per cent in the rider's head and 20 per cent in the machine,' he says. 'So if your rider wants gold handlebars, you give him gold handlebars.' Or you do if he knows what he's talking about and Burgess had already sussed that Valentino knows exactly what he was talking about. 'There are some riders who don't know what they want, they ask for stuff simply out of the frustration of not obtaining decent lap times; so you could move the geometry all around and then nobody knows what's going on. The old KISS principle doesn't work too badly on a motorcycle: keep it simple, stupid.' Burgess is an arch-pragmatist. While some rival engineers vainly attempt to reinvent the wheel to give their rider an advantage, he stays firmly grounded in the realms of the possible, his fundamental attitude to his job summed up by his father's racing principle, the five Ps: perfect preparation prevents poor performance.

But Valentino's astounding gift for understanding and analysing machine performance was about to show Burgess that the realms of the possible could be expanded. At Le Mans, all second-gear hairpins, he spirited himself through the pack after a so-so start, setting a new lap record as he caught leaders Roberts, Criville and Yamaha's Norick Abe. This was his first time properly up front and his first real opportunity to compare himself to his rivals and their machines. 'Valentino really started to talk about the bike after Le Mans. He said that where Alex had wheelspin, he also had wheelspin, but at that same point Abe's Yamaha would still be driving forward with traction. That's when we started the ball rolling for the NV4A, the derivative NSR which we used for the last few races of 2000, which developed into the NV4B he used throughout 2001.'

Two weeks later was the biggest day of his life: the Italian GP at Mugello and his first premier-class race on home tarmac. Whole hillsides tinged yellow by his fans, outbreaks of Biaggi red here and there. Valentino's shaky start was fast being forgotten by the media who were now salivating at the prospect of the first Rossi versus Biaggi duel. Whoever was writing the script was doing a great job: two Italian fighters set for a home-town brawl, no, make that three, Capirossi was up there too. One nation, three gladiators.

Qualifying was super close, the trio split by 0.132 seconds: Biaggi second, Rossi third, Capirossi fourth, Alex Barros on pole. The race was even closer, the trio trading blows out front, no doubt about it, this was going to end in tears. One and a half laps to go and Valentino hit the attack button, slid into the lead, then lost the front and fell at the next turn. Doohan, recently appointed HRC general manager to keep an eye on Honda's young chargers, had seen it all coming:

'He started riding the bike like it was a 250, running pretty deep into corners so he just got in there too hot and loaded up the front.'

Biaggi lasted another lap before colliding with Capirossi and falling, leaving Capirex to cruise across the line. Burgess had found the entire weekend an enlightening experience. 'I was unaware of what the Max/Valentino thing was about, I pretty much thought it was a media thing. I didn't know that Italy only became a country in 1871, so a lot of the regions still don't like each other.' Too right, it's Italy's north–south divide, the mezzogiorno, one of the reasons the pair are apparently irreconcilable. Biaggi is Roman, he's old-school Italian, resides in Monaco and has tea with the Pope; Valentino is from the Marches region, he's new-skool Italian, hangs out in London and goes clubbing with his mates.

So their first clash had ended nil-all; it wouldn't be their last. From now on every time they were in the same room together, usually only when duty called for pre- and post-race press conferences, the air crackled with animosity. Words would not be spoken, their eyes would never meet, and yet somehow they managed to keep a lid on it for another year.

At Catalunya Valentino rode his first wet 500 race, easing home third like he'd been doing it all his life, and remember this was the man who hated riding 'under the water'. Thirteen years earlier three-time 500 champ Wayne Rainey had ridden his first wet 500 GP, watched by his father. Sandy was awestruck, petrified by these meanest of machines, 'these things that don't even want you on their backs,' as he called them. True, rain tyres and digitally controlled power curves had come a long way since '88 and Catalunya's designer turns aren't the cold-steel lined sweepers of Spa, but this was another moment that history seemed to whisper his name. While all around people were losing their heads – the race turned into something of a crash fest – Valentino kept his, gleefully juggling the throttle, twisting his NSR sideways out of the turns.

At Assen he came in sixth after threatening the leaders before the rain came down. Two weeks later at Donington, more rain, for this was the year that swollen grey clouds followed the circus everywhere. Using wets on a drying track, Valentino jostled with championship leader Roberts and Jeremy McWilliams, smokin' his overheating rear tyre as he launched out of turns to win by a fraction. His first 500 victory had hardly come as a surprise.

His next ride, to second at the Sachsenring, was even more impressive. He may have been learning the art of 500 riding with astounding speed but he still hadn't acquired the ability to launch a 190hp/130kg motorcycle from the grid, a delicate balancing act requiring immaculate throttle/clutch interaction. Too much throttle, too much clutch and it's loop-the-loop time, too little and you get wasted on the dash to turn one. Valentino got destroyed, 16th at the end of the first lap, and this at a tortuous track where it's reckoned there's little or no room for overtaking. So he made some, conjuring lines that others seemed incapable of using, making fools of 500 racing's great and good as he picked them off wherever he pleased. With five laps to go he was ahead, then he bungled the final lap, crossing the line eight hundredths behind Barros.

'I'm very used to coming from the back because I've never been a very good starter, it was the same in 125 and 250. Like at Barcelona 2001, I started from pole but was almost last at the first corner after I collide with someone. Maybe other riders would have thought "Oh fack, we're lost", but I did the same in 250 there in '99 and the same at Sachsenring in 2000, just stay calm and go. It's always been quite easy for me to overtake anywhere, but I don't think that's because I'm better than the other guys, just because I try. Many other riders say that it's very hard to overtake at the Sachsenring, okay so it is, but if you try, maybe it's not very hard.' If only it was that easy for everyone.

After Germany the little matter of the Suzuka Eight Hours. This classic event, acted out in Japan's high summer of withering 35° heat and 80 per cent humidity, is the most important event in the world to Honda because of its influence on the massive domestic bike market. The roll call of winners includes illustrious names like Doohan, Rainey, Gardner and Eddie Lawson, all of them former 500 kings. But most GP riders loathe the race, finding it an awkward distraction from the real job of winning the World Championship. Not only can the switch to unfamiliar four-stroke machinery affect their 500 riding, but the factories' obsession with winning the event demands their stars' presence at pre-event tests. Poor Valentino had to go to Japan not once but twice during the five weeks preceding the race, delivering two doses of strength-sapping jetlag. Then again, he had asked for it. While Doohan had spent years fighting to get the Eight Hours scrubbed from his HRC contract, Valentino had volunteered for the job. 'I always love Eight Hours from when I was young because I love the Japanese colours and graphics. When I was at Aprilia I push very hard with Jan Witteveen (Aprilia's technical chief) to race an RSV Mille there. Also I want to try a Superbike, I want to ride with Superbike riders, see their level.'

So here was another question: okay, so he could ride 125, 250 and 500 two-strokes but how would he cope with the very different demands of a four-stroke? This wasn't merely idle contemplation, there was a crucial significance to his Eight Hour performance because GP racing was awaiting a landmark shift in technical regulations. From 2002 the premier class would be going four-stroke.

Surprise, surprise, Valentino had little trouble adapting to the factory SP-1 Superbike he'd share with race partner Colin

Edwards, who went on to win the 2000 World Supers crown. He found the softer, heavier SP-1 easy to ride and deceptively quick. 'The bike is incredible, it feels slow but the lap time is almost the same as with the NSR. You can ride the Superbike at 100 per cent all the time, is easy. With 500 you can ride it 100 per cent maybe three or four times a season, and when you use the 500 at 100 per cent, it's not like different class, it's like different sport.' Is easy but not that easy – Vale and his American team-mate led the race, then they had a crash each. Situation normal: new bike, necessary find limit.

Already GP racing's biggest star, he was downgraded to non-person for the next GP at Brno. Vale had left his passport at home, so he smuggled himself over the Czech border, competing as an illegal alien. Not that anyone seemed to notice, let alone care. Second there and third in Portugal he now found himself hauling in points leader Roberts. With three races to go he was 46 points behind the son of a legend, a long call but not impossible. Was he about to change the habit of a lifetime and win something at the first attempt?

It seemed unlikely, since he was happy to admit that he was still struggling to get the hang of riding a 500 and even more so the labyrinthine art of refining the bike's settings to suit his style. 'I still have problems understanding the 500, I still can't use 100 per cent of the bike,' he said in Portugal. What he really wanted was to ride a 500 like his childhood heroes, the 'Old Dogs' as he called them, brave men like Schwantz, Doohan, Rainey and Gardner who raced with reckless throttle hands, kicking out the bike's ass end and getting 'kinda squirrelly'. 'They were the true 500 riders and my dream is to use a 500 like those guys.'

He'd get there very soon but not just yet. His title charge ended in the gravel at Valencia after he'd teetered on the brink once too often, asking too much edge grip from the front tyre, still riding the thing like it was a 250. He effectively crashed twice in the race, except he somehow managed to save the first. This was Vale in rare rostrum-or-hospital mode. Burgess: 'He pretty much knew that if he didn't beat Roberts there then the title was gone. If he had beaten him there he could've kept the title open right to the last race, that was the way he saw it.'

Down in Rio he bounced back with his first dry-weather 500 win, dismissing Barros, McCoy, Abe and Biaggi with a new-found confidence – he'd finally managed to kick his 250 habits and start riding the NSR like a true 500 rider. 'In Rio we change my style very much because I basically crash two times at Valencia, the first, whooooa,' he says, doing a very passable imitation of his big sideways moment. 'The second I crash, so I speak with Jeremy, we watch the Rio race on TV and I finally understand that I need to change my riding style because I make very much crash with the front tyre. Until this race I was quite fast but I ride like 250, so I always finish the front tyre after half the race.'

So Valentino adapted his cornering lines. He reduced the arc of corner entry, lowering his mid-corner speed and focusing all his efforts into a straight drive out of the turn. That way he could lay down as much horsepower as his rear Michelin would allow and a little bit more, using the wheelspin to get sideways, pointing his NSR's front end back towards the inside of the corner, tightening his line and giving him more room to get on the gas, which means more speed down the next straight. It's something like using the handbrake in a car, except he uses the throttle to break traction, rather than the brake.

'The perfect line is stay wide, wide, wide and after you close the line and go in inside, slowing a little bit to the apex. With the 250 it's possible to do this and if you make like this with the 500 you are very fast but when you go to close the line after seven laps you lose the front and you crash. So necessary go inside a little bit early and a little bit more, use less speed in the corner and after pick up the bike and accelerate. So I change very much the first part of the corner. Not so much the second part because when I ride 250 I already ride a little bit like 500, picking up the bike to accelerate, more than other 250 riders. In Rio I begin to use less speed in the corner and start to spin the rear tyre very much on the exit.

'For many years I train for spinning with motocross bike because sliding and spinning is also very much fun. But spinning was impossible with the 250 because not enough power, so when I arrive in 500 I want to try and I get better and better. In winter I still train on the dirt, using a motocross front tyre and trail-bike rear tyre with little grip, so I'm sideways all the time, this gives me a big help for learning to slide the 500.'

Like Donington there were no comedy post-race gags at Rio, just a loving hug for his NSR. By now they were the best of mates, and if investing an inanimate object with life sounds nuts, it isn't, it helps cement that man–machine bond so crucial in racing. During 2000 Vale flaunted their thriving relationship with the post-race rolling burn-out, a tricky stunt that became his favourite way of telling the world what a laugh he was having out there. 'The 250 never had enough power but it's sweet on the 500, you just spin the tyre till it gets hot and there's no grip, then you only need a little throttle. I like it very much.'

Onward to Motegi for the Pacific GP where he couldn't catch a runaway Roberts but did defeat Biaggi in a last-lap duel, their first serious encounter since Mugello. 'Passing him,' he said afterwards. 'Was like the best orgasm.' One-nil. But Biaggi had his revenge two weeks later, brave winner of an epic season-ending Australian GP, Capirossi second, Vale third, the three of them separated by just two tenths. He ended the championship second behind Roberts, although there was no doubt who'd been strongest in the later stages of the 16-round series. And if he hadn't crashed out of those first two races ...

Winter was dedicated to perfecting the NV4A prototype he had raced for the first time at Valencia, refining the chassis, cylinders, ignition mapping and carburettors. This bike was tailor made for Valentino, according to his desire for improved rear-end traction, because now there was no doubt who was HRC's number one. 'It was the first time HRC had really changed the NSR's chassis since '91,' says Burgess. 'They were ecstatic they'd got a guy with new ideas.'

In between test sessions in Australia, Malaysia and Europe Vale got on with the rest of his life: snowboarding with mates, doing some rallying and moving to London. He rented a West-End apartment in the British capital because he needed to get out of Italy but couldn't handle the thought of moving to Monaco, the VIP ghetto that is home to so many GP riders, F1 drivers and other chinless tax exiles. 'I could live there for two days, but after that? Is not the real world.' London is the real world, urban mayhem and gridlock, so he blagged an SP-1 and a FireBlade from Honda UK, then settled on a less hectic CBR600. Most of all though he was having fun descending into London clubland with his mates who were taking it in turns flying over from Italy to help him party. In October he had split up with longtime girlfriend Eliane Ferni so he was out on the loose, often at the upmarket China White Club near Piccadilly which counts Prince Andrew amongst its other clientele. Oh well, you can't have everything.

Chapter 6

WINNING VERY MUCH

Pre-ride rituals are vital to racers. They provide an ordered system of preparation devoid of the unforeseen, so the rider can maintain his focus on his machine and retain all his mental capacity to deal with whatever mayhem might be unleashed on the racetrack. Like most racers, Valentino's pre-ride ritualism has little to do with superstition; how could any serious racer believe that the outcome of a race might depend on how he slips on his gloves? No, it's just a procedure that allows him to prepare as perfectly as possible for each outing. Through order comes calm, so his leathers and back protector are always laid out in the same neat arrangement in the team truck and his helmet and gloves are always to be found in the same place in the pits. It's the only sure-fire way of avoiding the kind of 'Where the fack are my gloves?' nonsense that might distract his mind or threaten his cool at such a vital moment.

His pre-ride routine is renowned, the TV cameras apparently endlessly fascinated by the process, which goes something like this: wet his fingers, massage eyes, fiddle with earring, pull on helmet, slip on gloves, walk towards bike, bend forward, squat down, grasp right footpeg – apparently performing some kind of communion with the motorcycle – climb aboard, tug bum of leathers while riding down pit-lane.

'When I make like this,' he smiles, grabbing the crotch of his jeans, 'is only to make sure my leather are in the right position, is not superstition, if you want perfect leather for riding they're too baggy before you ride. Is the same with the squat, just to stretch the leather. The eye massage is because it's better for looking and I always touch my earring because, well, now is impossible to stop, is habit. For sure this also is not only superstition. If I know exactly where my things are it gives me a feeling of calm and security, so I can think only about the bike. At races I always arrive in the pit at the last moment, so if all is okay the time is enough, but if not I need more time and for sure I'm late to ride. I'm like this also when I'm away from the races, when possible I stay very organised.'

The regularity extends to Valentino's working days – Fridays, Saturdays and Sundays. 'Every day is the same. I go to bed around one and wake up eight-thirty, make the shower and make the breakfast: tea, biscuit and coffee. Then go to the pits, go in the team truck where I have my leather and everything and always music. The truck is office, the motorhome is home and always full because there's always someone staying. First practice and also race warm-up begin at ten and after I speak with my mechanics and eat at noon, then go to make massage at the Clinica Mobile where they put Chinese deep-heat tape on my arms to make my muscles work better and to stop pump-up. Qualifying and race is at two and after I speak to Jeremy and have interview with all the journalists. When all is finished after practice I rest in my motorhome for one hour, listen to music, use my Playstation, then go and eat. After that I usually make sticker for my bike. When I was young I did all the stickers on my bikes, now I just do The Doctor, number 46, my own sticker. Then maybe spend the evening talking with friends about ... nothing!'

Burgess has seen it all before: 'Valentino's method of operation is the same all the time, just like any professional sportsman's should be. Mick used to do it, he used to spend minutes and minutes putting his gloves on. It was a concentration thing, leaving one world behind and preparing to enter another. A racer ambles around the paddock at a few kays, then he's doing speeds of 300kmh, so he's got to have his wits around him. All the ritual stuff is like a buffer zone between those two worlds, it puts the rider's mind in gear before he gets on the bike.'

Valentino's post-ride ritual is just as crucial to his race-day performance. He keeps to a strict debrief regime with JB and his crew. 'After practice we sit in the pits for ten minutes and he'll go through what happened in that session,' says Burgess. 'Then he'll talk to Juan (Martinez, Showa suspension technician) and me, making a lap on a circuit map, telling us what's happening with the bike. During that first conversation I'll ask him if we'll be changing the gearbox or anything else major, so we can do a certain amount of work before he comes back at six-ish when he talks with Juan and myself again, and within 20 minutes we've got it all done.

'Valentino uses his head, he thinks and he thinks and he thinks. He was great from the moment he started working with us at the end of '99, but there was a big change in him from 2000 to 2001, like he was coming out of being a teenager and becoming a man. In 2000 everything had been pretty spontaneous, in 2001 things were more methodical and thought out, more of the brain side coming in. I get the feeling he now feels he's an adult in an adult's world, while the previous five years of his career had just been good fun.'

Valentino agrees that his attitude to life has changed over the past few years. 'The way you see things, your view of the world, changes between the ages of 18 and 22,' he says. 'I'm older now, so I think I understand more, and for sure my life has changed. When you're 16 or 17 you don't have problems, unless it's something really big like family problems. Life is different when you're young, you only really think about having fun.'

Riding the 500 changed him too, from boy to man. The daft victory celebrations faded into memory as a new-found seriousness took hold. He was growing up anyway and there was no way he could remain unaffected by the pressures of competing in racing's biggest class on the scariest race bikes known to man. 'The jokes also stop because I don't think a lot of people really understood the whole thing. It's like Mugello 2001 when we had my bikes painted Hawaii style. When I crashed people said I only crashed because I'd been up all night painting them! So I decided it was better to stop all this and just wave like other riders, then have a big party on Sunday night with my real friends.' Plus he had new responsibilities helping Honda develop two amazing motorcycles, the last-of-the-line NSR500 and the RC211V, HRC's V5 weapon for the new four-stroke MotoGP class.

All this was reflected by a change in alter ego for 2001: exit Paparinik, enter The Doctor. 'We change because with 500s you don't need a superhero, you just need to be quiet, calm and thoughtful, more like a doctor,' he explains. 'Also, because in Italy there are very many doctors called Dr Rossi, so I became Dr Rossi.' The new nickname could hardly have been more apt, because he began 2001 in immaculate style, winning the first three races with surgical precision.

The season began at Suzuka, the circuit that Soichiro Honda built in 1962, where success means so much to the world's biggest bike brand. And this time more than ever. Honda had won a total of 497 World Championship races since their first GP win in 1961, so a full house of 125, 250 and 500 victories at Suzuka would give them their 500th success. But it had been well over a year since they had won all three races in one day, so it seemed an impossible dream that Honda would attain the magic number on cherished home tarmac. Especially since their 125s were well off the pace in qualifying.

'It was a Honda fantasy that they win their 500th race on that day,' Vale recalls. 'It was incredible, we watched the other races on TV and I say: 'For sure Honda won't win 125,' but fack, Azuma wins, then in 250 Kato wins, so fack, I must win 500.' And win he did, recovering from a scary 120mph collision with Biaggi to beat McCoy by less than a second and trigger massive celebrations within Honda. The Midas touch once again.

This was another of those days that had one idly wondering if the boy is perhaps blessed or if there's wizardry afoot in his life. Valentino's career was apparently evolving into an implausible plot for a cheesy Hollywood racetrack drama, *Days of Thunder* style. Anyone could have won Honda's 500th Grand Prix victory and it could have happened in any class at any track, but it didn't, it was Rossi, in the premier 500 class and at Suzuka.

The suggestion that greater forces might be at work in his life would keep returning throughout the next 12 months or so, not that they'd been entirely absent in previous years. At Donington in July he suffered a massive 125mph get-off during practice and walked away to win the race. Three years earlier the same corner had almost claimed Checa's life. During August's Czech GP at Brno a bee flew inside his helmet, flew out again and he rode on to win the race. British 500 rider Leon Haslam suffered the same fate that weekend with very different consequences; he got stung and went blind in one eye, forcing him into the pits. By the end of the season Valentino had also won the closest 500 GP in history, at Phillip Island, and the final race of the 500 era at Rio, where a conveniently placed backmarker helped him beat Checa at the very last turn. Then he began the new age of four-strokes with victory at the 2002 Japanese GP, making it look too easy on a flooded Suzuka track, like he was walking on water. And to think, his father looks like Jesus ...

Of course, you can attribute much of Valentino's success and apparent luck to his genius, but there's little doubt that he seems to enjoy more than his fair share of historical coincidences and lucky escapes. Some people are just like that, when things go right, they keep going right. Or as Eddie Lawson once said: 'The more I practise, the luckier I get'.

Wins at Welkom and Jerez completed the hat-trick and these were dominant victories achieved at a dizzying speed, race records smashed at every track. Valentino was forcing the 500 pace for the first time since Doohan had disappeared, helped along by a new generation of Michelin slicks. He had quickly realised that the French company's 16.5-inch rear tyre offered much better grip at the end of races, so he made the effort to adapt his settings to suit the tyre's different profile, while some of his rivals stuck with the easier-handling 17-inch tyre and paid the price at the end of races. Once again he was proving himself to be receptive to new ideas, all he wanted was speed, it didn't much matter what the bike felt like. 'After Mick stopped the 500 pace was always slow. I hated that, so it was time to raise the pace.'

And there were few that could run with him: Capirossi a lone and firmly defeated rival at Welkom, and no one to play with at Jerez after he'd finished toying with Abe. Valentino, like Doohan before him, was going quicker and quicker, the pack scattered behind him, and for a while it looked like 500 racing might return to those oh-so predictable Doohan days, when everyone awoke on Sundays with just one question on their minds: who'll get second?

Doohan, a hard man to impress but mellowing in retirement, was moved to fulsome praise by his protégé's lightning form. 'He's riding the bike like it should be ridden and he doesn't feel there's any reward in just running around with the pack. Some of the other guys have been caught out a little and guys like Max need to learn to ride the bike when it's not 100 per cent. When everything's good, Max is quick but when things aren't right ...'

At Le Mans things did come right for Biaggi and he inflicted a major defeat on Valentino, who was pushed into third by

Checa but still managed to tip his deadly rival a contemptuous wink on the podium. Cheeky. This was the start of Biaggi's tilt at the title. The Roman's technicians had made a crucial forward jump with machine settings, and when Valentino crashed out of the rain-lashed Italian GP, his arch-rival took another chunk out of his points lead. In the space of three races his advantage over Biaggi had shrunk from 46 to 21 points and tension was building. At Catalunya it exploded, the pair going for each others' throats in a cramped ante room after the race, which Vale had won in masterful style, recovering from a disastrous start to pick off his rivals and leave them trailing, Capirossi second, Biaggi third. The punch up between these two pumped up racers had been brewing for years, though it was more of an unseemly brawl than a man-to-man duel. There is no impartial record of exactly what happened because the pair were out of view when the fight kicked off, on their way to the post-race TV interview room with their various hangers-on.

'What happened wasn't very big and it wasn't important,' insists Valentino. 'It was like being at school: "He started it!" "No, he started it!" "No, he started it!" Biaggi said that I started this facking shit but it's necessary to think about what happened before. I started the race from last position and I arrived first at the flag, I made the fastest lap and I made a fantastic victory, so why would I want to make all that shit?'

According to one witness, Biaggi did manage to headbutt Valentino's team manager Carlo Fiorani while his arms were behind his back. Then he managed to fight free, clocking his nemesis in the face. If you were looking for a points decision in the absence of a knockout you'd probably give the fight to Mighty Max who won more cred in the post-race press conference when quizzed about his grazed face. 'A mosquito bit me,' he replied. The incident uncovered a streak of dignity within the older Italian, who was quick to remind everyone that he'd never stoked the fires of the long-running feud. 'My only defence is to say nothing,' he said, well aware of the difficulties of a PR offensive against everyone's favourite GP racer. All he did say was that Valentino only whacked him while Fiorani had his arms behind his back: 'That wasn't nice, it was unfair.'

Biaggi insists he's baffled by the rivalry. 'We only started racing together in 2000 but it feels like Rossi's been racing me ever since he was in 125s. It's not normal to have a go at another rider when you're not even in the same class. Rossi is clever, he gets energy from all this, but I think people get tired of it.' Of course, people weren't getting tired of it. This was more fun than anyone had had for years: a real, genuine confrontation between two riders who hate each other's guts. Somehow it makes the racing more real, more urgent.

Two weeks later at Assen the pair were brought together to shake hands in front of the cameras, a feat they managed without once looking into each other's eyes. The forced smiles did nothing to soothe their antagonism or hush the apoplectic Italian media, but at least they'd made the effort to convince people that they weren't out to kill each other at this most frightening of racetracks.

Valentino reckons that Assen features the most challenging corner in GP racing, Hoge Heide, where riders must tackle successive waves of camber while negotiating a 160mph right–left flick near the end of the lap. Through the right they ride into a deep dip, suspension fully compressed, before rising out of the dip and heaving the bike left as the suspension fully extends. A moment of deathly silence follows, riders apparently in cruise mode, unable to do anything because the bike is just floating across the tarmac with no grip, so any input would almost certainly cause a big, big crash. But as soon as they descend from that final wave of camber the suspension loads up and they flick into the

110mph Ramshoek left. It's an impressive sight in qualifying when riders are mostly alone, putting their all into one perfect lap, but in the race, with Vale, Biaggi, Capirossi and Barros locked together in a vicious dogfight, it was frankly terrifying. Someone up there must've known this confrontation might end in disaster, so down came the rain and out came the red flags. Biaggi had been ahead the lap before the race was stopped and was thus declared the winner, Valentino second, Capirossi third.

Robbed of victory and now only 19 points ahead, Valentino and crew headed across the Channel for the British GP where things went from bad to worse. That huge tumble in qualifying left him a dismal 11th on the grid, Max sitting pretty on pole. In the race he bided his time, waiting for the fuel load to lighten before relentlessly working his way toward the front. Race leader Biaggi must've got the shock of his life when his pit board told him who was behind him and within a few laps he too succumbed. At such a crucial stage of the season, when lesser racers might've settled for safe points rather than a risky ride to the front, this was a truly inspired ride. And it's right up there in Vale's all-time best races. 'Maybe this was my most exciting victory because I didn't think it was possible to win, so when I crossed the finish line it was the most emotion for me.'

To Japan for Eight Hours tests and then to Germany, where he was back to earth with a bump. If the 2001 NSR was a magnificent motorcycle it soon became obvious that it didn't like the Sachsenring's tortuous twists. Once again he qualified 11th but this time there was no Lazarus-style comeback and he finished the race a crestfallen seventh. Biaggi won at a canter, leading home three other Yamahas, the YZR's sweet-handling chassis lapping up the German curves. Now there were just ten points between them, and all of a sudden the clever money was on Biaggi who had won three of his four 250 titles with storming end-of-season flourishes, while Vale had never been involved in a bruising fight to the finish.

But no time for wailing and gnashing of teeth, just another 12-hour plane ride to Suzuka where he and Edwards made no mistakes second time around, winning the Eight Hours and returning to the circuit the next morning for something much more important: Valentino's first ride on the all-new RC211V. With Biaggi's YZR500 in the ascendance, here at least was something that might give him some cheer for the future. Not so, Vale declared the test 'a disaster' and returned home to psyche himself up for the Czech GP. In all kinds of ways this would be a crucial encounter. Brno commences the second half of the season after GP racing's summer recess and performances at this epic, high-speed circuit are invariably a good forecast for the remainder of the campaign. During the summer holidays some riders mysteriously fall out of the groove, while others find the speed missing from their earlier outings. So from a purely psychological standpoint it was vital for both riders that they win here. No wonder Valentino considers it the most difficult race of his life.

Ever the master of the artfully fast one-off lap, Biaggi claimed pole, just over a tenth up on Valentino, then led the race, his rival quickly slotting in behind. That's how they stayed for some while, Valentino watching and waiting, gathering the information he'd require for an end-of-race attack. 'Biaggi was going so quick and I was thinking, "Ah, maybe it's possible to overtake him here on the last lap", or "Here I'm faster, there I'm slower", and when he crashed I thought "Oh fack, now it's necessary to change my plan".' Biaggi had skated over the edge of the precipice, losing the front and sliding gracefully to earth, then remounting in a panic to salvage a handful of points for tenth. They hardly mattered. The gap was back to 29 points and the scene had been set for the final six races.

'I think Brno is the masterpiece of my career because the mental situation was so difficult before the race, though after Biaggi crashed it wasn't very much exciting.' He followed that with another untroubled win at Estoril where Biaggi covered himself in dust once more, clambering back on board to grimly keep himself on the scoring board. At Valencia Biaggi got his own back, beating Valentino by almost three seconds, but they were only racing for tenth place, the event turned into a tyre lottery by a pre-race downpour.

Leaving Europe behind for the final four 'flyaway' races the gap had swollen to 47 points but Biaggi was not for giving in. He led Valentino at Motegi, only to stumble over the limit once more. Biaggi's pride had been pricked by the run of calamities and turned his wrath not against Valentino but against Yamaha. The YZR chassis, he announced, had a 'structural problem' which didn't allow him to ride as fast as he wanted. He had already complained that Rossi always got lucky, always got the best bikes, conveniently forgetting that he too had been favoured with NSR500 power in '98. But that year he had been in a satellite Honda team and had complained once too often that his equipment didn't match up to Doohan's factory tackle. After that HRC weren't keen to promote him to official team duties, so he decided to switch factories.

Valentino, of course, saw it all differently. There had been no crisis at Yamaha, rather Vale and his crew had been shaken into getting their act together following their disastrous Sachsenring weekend. 'After Germany I told him we wouldn't tolerate the second or third rows anymore,' reveals Burgess. 'I told him he was making great entertainment for the fans but if he wanted to win the championship he'd have to put some pressure on his rival and it's hard to do that from the third row. After that we were only off the front row once all year. We also changed a lot during the next few races: shocks, suspension links, geometry, engine bits, everything, which allowed us to make big improvements in handling.' That's why Biaggi could no longer hack the pace.

'The better parts from HRC helped but it was the team that made the difference because they changed their way of working to suit me,' adds Valentino. 'I use more corner speed than Doohan and you need more accurate settings to ride with my style. So all the suspension settings changed and the bike started to turn better. The Honda 500 had always had a turning problem, it would always run wide, but it was better after Germany.'

Three races to go and the title would be his if he could make the top eight at Phillip Island. Oooh, too tough. Indeed it was, of all the races in which he might have been granted an easy ride, this wasn't it. Phillip Island's fast, swooping curves always encourage elbow-to-elbow racing, but the 2001 Australian GP was an epic amongst Aussie epics, the closest race in over half a century of 500 racing, almost too close. During the early laps Barros and Nori Haga scared the living daylights out of everyone as they duked it out for the lead, Valentino deciding the only safe place was out front after he'd kissed tyres with Barros at 190mph. He didn't stay there long, barging back and forth with Biaggi, Capirossi, Jacque, Nakano and Ukawa. On the final lap it was Max out front by a smidgen but Valentino timed his move to perfection, diving ahead with three corners to go. Less than two seconds separated the first nine riders past the flag, so tactical riding had never been an option and anyway, riding for points isn't his style. Roberts and Criville had won their crowns by doing no more than was absolutely necessary and he wasn't about to emulate them. Burgess, like everyone, was mightily impressed: 'I've always said that if you win races the championships take care of themselves. It's always been that way with the guys I've worked with – Mick, Gardner and Spencer, they all knew how to fight.'

Back home in Tavullia it was almost 6am and the exultant locals were painting the town yellow. Mum wasn't with them though, she'd made the long trip Down Under to celebrate her boy's conquest of motorcycling's highest peak, just 22 years and 240 days after she'd first laid eyes on him.

Valentino isn't the youngest rider to have won the 500 crown, however. Three others have managed it even younger: Freddie Spencer won the 1983 title at 21 years and 258 days, Mike Hailwood secured the 1962 crown aged 22 and 160 days and John Surtees took the 1956 championship at 22 years and 182 days. So what's so special about these guys? What unites them? Riding talent, for a start, towering mountains and raging rivers of the stuff, plus total, unfaltering dedication. (Surtees called his own brand of world-beating determination, 'the inherent Surtees family cussedness'.) And dads that raced bikes: Spencer Senior raced just about anything – dirt bikes, drag bikes, sprint cars, even powerboats – while Hailwood's old man and Surtees' dad raced sidecars before the Second World War. In other words, it all comes down to nature and nurture.

After watching the race in his pyjamas at home, Graziano may well have been pondering this very subject as he popped down the local *barbiere* to have his pony tail cut off in celebration. The cherished pony had been growing ever since he'd emerged shaven-headed from his career-ending coma in September 1982 and here at last was a good enough reason to get rid of the thing. 'It wasn't for a bet, just a display of appreciation and affection,' explains Graziano. 'I told him I'd cut it off if he won all three titles. Every time he's passed to a higher level it's been a pleasurable surprise for me. When he won his first GP in '96 that didn't mean he'd be good at 250s, and 500s are a whole different thing again, so I only realised he's really, really good when he won the 500 championship.'

Moving swiftly on to Sepang the following weekend, Valentino might have been tempted to kick back in the stultifying tropical heat and luxuriate in the glory of it all. Not so, he made the rest look second-rate with a runaway win, having big fun spinning his hot and greasy Michelins well ahead of Capirossi. Incredibly, this was the moment that Valentino reckons he finally mastered the 500: 'In Malaysia I finally arrive to go very fast with the 500.' And this 38th win took him into the all-time top nine GP winners' list.

Just one race to go before the end of the 500 era and surely there was only one man who should win it. But conditions could scarcely have been trickier at Rio, the rain coming and going, Valentino crossing the finish line second, a fraction down on Checa, but still winning. How so? The race had been interrupted by a rain shower and run in two parts, the result decided on aggregate. Valentino crossed the finish line a metre behind the Spaniard but had a two tenths advantage in hand from the first leg. To add indignity to defeat, he'd done it running the wrong tyres – squirming intermediates against his rival's noticeably grippier cut slicks. Chubby Checa's look of abject misery upon the podium spoke for everyone: 'Just what do we have to do to beat this guy?'

Of course, there was one man he'd never beaten – Doohan. So could he beat the biggest, baddest of the Old Dogs? 'I've seen some of Mick's data readouts and, fack, he was very fast. It was him that made the difference, not the bike. If I was to race Mick, I think I could fight with him, but I don't know who would win. Nobody knows!' Burgess also sits on the fence on this one: 'I wouldn't like to say Valentino's got more talent than Mick, I've seen Mick do some pretty special things on a motorcycle.'

And what if Valentino rode a Yamaha, could he still beat Max? 'Biaggi gave 120 per cent to beat me in 2001, so the fight was facking hard. In the past he never rode the 500 like that.

For me, I think I could beat him with Yamaha because we're not talking about Biaggi winning six races and me seven, or me scoring just ten points more than him. Of course, I think my bike is very good, but I also think that I was the fastest rider of 2001, usually. I won 11 races, Biaggi won three and he only won Assen because the race was stopped early. And when he won at Le Mans and Sachsenring his team-mate Checa was second, so for sure those tracks were not so bad for the Yamaha; at Sachsenring there were five Yamahas in the first six!'

Not that the relative differences between the YZR and NSR mattered any more, because 500s were about to be consigned to history, although Valentino wasn't happy about that because he didn't reckon the RCV was going to be as fun to ride. In fact he kept suggesting he might stick with the NSR in 2002, although he was only kidding himself. Honda had been a prime mover in the shift to four-strokes, so there was no way they were going to let their number one rider continue racing a 'stinkwheel'.

RCV testing began alongside new team-mate Ukawa at Phillip Island in November and then at Jerez, a whole army of HRC engineers descending on the Andalucian track, praying that the work they'd done since July would be to their champion's liking. It wasn't. 'The problem was that the Japanese testers who did the first riding would never say "This is shit", they just say "Yes, this is quite good", so when I arrive the bike has big problems. To make better, you must say "This is good, or this is shit". The bike still wasn't very good at Jerez but we made a good test there. I'm good at understanding what I want from the bike and HRC are very good at giving me what I want. After Jerez everything changed: the cowling, the seat, the engine character, all the electronic parts, it was a new bike by the start of the 2002 season.'

In other words, maybe the RCV wouldn't have become the weapon it did without Valentino's unique input. Your average rider works on machine set-up one adjustment at a time, so if the bike turns better, keeps its line better or is more stable, he'll know what caused that improvement, so his crew can make further adjustments in that direction and perhaps make the bike even better. If his crew were to change several things at once – say one click on the front rebound damping, two clicks on the rear compression and a different construction front tyre – the rider couldn't be sure which of these changes affected performance, so his crew can't go on from there. Valentino is different. 'He has some kind of amazing link system which allows him to think "I like this" and "I don't like this",' explains Fiorani. 'So he can test many different things at the same time without getting confused.' This is just another part of his talent for riding a motorcycle ridiculously fast – it's not just riding ability, it's his pit-lane brain that helps him improve the bike, so he can employ even more of his talent on the track.

During the Jerez tests Valentino did at least break his own 500 record, although recently crowned 250 champ Daijiro Kato was also there, getting into the swing of things with his NSR500s, and he went even faster. This was the first hint that the two-strokes might not roll over and die the moment the four-strokes hit the track. Ever since Checa had ridden Yamaha's YZR-M1 four-stroke to a blindingly fast simulated race time during private tests at Brno in August, the 500s had looked dead and gone. But here was evidence to suggest that reports of their demise had been greatly exaggerated. Around tighter and slower tracks the four-strokes seemed unable to fully exploit their 200-plus horsepower engines while the two-strokes could capitalise on their lighter weight.

Four wheels were next, and he put on an impressive display in Michelin's Race of Champions rally event on Gran Canaria where he made it to the quarter finals, only losing out to World Rally star Alistair McRae. People were already suggesting he'd quit bikes in a year or two to go full-time rallying. 'If I win with the four-stroke maybe it will be necessary to change sport and, after bikes, rallying is my passion, but to say I'll do the World Rally after bikes is unreal, because, fack, you have people who've been racing rallies for 25 years, while I'd be starting from zero, so I don't know if I can be fast enough.'

Of course, this wouldn't be the last we'd hear of four-wheel frolics. A year later panic would spread through bike racing's corridors of power as Rossi prepared for his WRC debut, driving a factory Peugeot 206 in the Rally of Great Britain. Some of the sport's bosses were deeply concerned at rumours of his defection to the car world, as if they believed bike racing might not even survive the departure of its biggest box-office draw. No sportsman can be bigger than the sport that made him, but with Valentino, it was beginning to look like a close run thing ...

Chapter 7

AND WHY THE LONG FACE?

Valentino's all-conquering 2001 campaign had proved to the world that he was more than just a 125 and 250 ace. He was, no doubt about it, the fastest motorcycle racer on earth, and now he wanted to be paid accordingly. At the end of 1999, when he did his first deal with Honda, he needed them as much as, and maybe more than, they had needed him. Now, as the two parties sat down to thrash out a new deal for 2002 and beyond, Valentino was king of racing's toughest class and he was sticking out for a fair rate for a job well done.

He had been due for his first ride of 2002 at Sepang in late January, where he was to check out HRC's latest refinements to the RCV. But the test never happened. Just after the New Year, the two parties fell out over the new two-year contract, reputed to be worth £10 million. In fact, he was happy with the cash – who wouldn't be? – but there were a number of detail clauses which caused him and manager Gibo some concern. 'In December, we understand we are still a little too far away, so we need time to change something in the contract about our point of view and something about Honda's point of view. But the biggest problem is that all the Italian journalist write too much; is not true that the argument was about Honda wanting me to use the number one, not 46. We had already finished that discussion before the end of 2001 season. No, we have other problem but is better we don't say; is secret.'

So Valentino was becoming something of a hard nut – as tough in the boardroom as he was on the racetrack. And he was different in public too. The more races he won, the further his fame spread, and however rich that was making him, the hassles of celebrity were really getting to him. 'Is very difficult to manage this because is very difficult to do everything that people want you to do. For sure, if I always finish in fifth place, we wouldn't have this problem! So is a good problem, but is still difficult.'

During 2002, Valentino's smile became more forced and less real, his eyes downcast as he wandered the paddock to avoid glances that might draw him into yet another autograph-signing session or the umpteenth meaningless chat of the day. In a society that worships celebrity like none other before it, Valentino was showing typical symptoms of overexposure. Then again, you could hardly blame him; some people were taking the piss, like MotoGP rights-holders Dorna who were working MotoGP's shining light big time. He was putting up with it, but then it all got too much at Assen, where Dorna had him visit a cheese factory for a pre-Dutch TT promo photo opportunity. Cheesy or what? A few years back, he would've gritted his teeth and laughed at the pointlessness of it all; now he was happy to tell the media what he thought of Dorna, and they weren't the only ones to cop a spray during 2002. While an uneasy truce prevailed with Biaggi, Valentino even had a pop at his team-mate Ukawa for having the audacity to overtake him at Sepang. Poor old Ukawa, possibly the most inoffensive man in the paddock. Yup, the wide-eyed teenage naivety had gone: now Valentino was a hard man in a hard world.

And this wasn't just in the little world of motorcycle racing. Rossi's name went mainstream during 2002, his grinning face filling billboards from Rio to Roppongi, flogging everything from jeans and sunglasses to motorcycles and engine oil. All nice easy money, but not that easy. Things had also changed in the big, bad real world, a growing inequality between cultures triggering terrorism, war and general instability. Even sportsmen couldn't escape reality, and just before Christmas 2002 Valentino was named in notes attached to a flurry of letter bombs mailed around Europe by a group of Repsol-hating anti-capitalists.

So he ended the year in hiding, just as he had started it, when he'd hunkered down with Gibo in London, firing off faxes and emails to HRC and working on his new look: shaggy-dog hair, bewhiskered face and a military green forage cap, like a youthful Fidel Castro. Very cool. 'I begin to look like a wolf and in March my mother say I can't come in her house!' He also acquired a deep tan from somewhere, certainly not from London's winter sun. 'Is not real sun, is lamp! My girls like it!' (Note the plural.) And we thought Biaggi was the vain one ...

The contract wrangle was resolved in time for the next tests at Sepang in early February, where he demolished the 500 lap and race records he'd established in October, giving HRC a timely reminder of his worth. News of the RCV's devastating speed raised blood pressure in race shops around Japan and Italy, especially in Iwata where Yamaha were toiling away on their M1. Biaggi and Checa had tested the M1 at Sepang during December and neither had gone as quick. But lap times exacted from private tests are often misleading because track conditions vary from day to day and because the numbers are often pure propaganda. So no one was quite sure whether HRC were giving it some spin, until the first group teams test at Catalunya in March, when Valentino came out well on top, Ukawa and Capirossi the only ones even close. And Capirossi was riding his 2001-spec NSR like a maniac: little body hunched forward, grimly hanging on as the bike took on a life of its own, all crossed up and pointing any which way but straight forward.

The same deal during final pre-season tests at Suzuka – Valentino well ahead and Capirossi already proclaiming him World Champion. 'Loris say that with the RCV I can win the title riding with one hand, maybe I will try,' joked Vale. Suzuka race weekend was no walkover, however. He crashed twice in practice, destroying one of his RCVs. This was surely a wake-up call for someone straying dangerously close to the foggy realm of over-confidence. The crashes were big ones, but he got away with both, like someone was still up there, looking out for him. On Friday, he lost the front at 120mph through the scary wall-lined right-hander after the hairpin, bloodying his hands as he scrubbed off speed before ricocheting off the trackside barriers. (The following year Marco Melandri crashed in exactly the same place and suffered a broken leg.) Then, the next morning, he took such a wide line into Degner that he ran off the track on the outside as he peeled in. This was playing way too fast and loose with his cornering lines.

Suitably chastened, he only just scraped into pole position, his rivals much closer than pre-season lap times had predicted. On the Sunday he rode a careful, well-thought-out race in sodden conditions, learning the best rain lines from local Suzuki rider Akira Ryo before moving ahead to narrowly win the first race of the new four-stroke era. Typical canny logic. He later considered this his best ride of the whole season: 'Suzuka was good for me because we stay there for two weeks to test the machine before the race – work, work, test, test, setting, setting – then Sunday morning – rain! Already I make two crashes, so the situation isn't easy for me, but we win the race.'

The victory was also Honda's first four-stroke GP success since their original racing era had ended in 1967, so not only was the shift of eras helping to build his legend, it was also making Honda love him even more. The newly appointed

HRC president Suguru Kanazawa emphasised the significance of the success: 'Winning GPs with four-stroke machinery has always been our goal, so this victory is very meaningful to me and everyone else at Honda'. Kanazawa had been working towards this day ever since he had left university in the late 1970s and designed the exotic, oval-pistoned NR500 four-stroke, which was humiliated by the then-dominant Yamaha and Suzuki two-strokes.

Suzuka, however, proved to be an inaccurate forecast for the season. The RCV was in fact much further ahead of its rivals than it had appeared there. Honda had moved things on with the V5. While rival manufacturers had, to a greater or lesser extent, continued down the same old GP road, wrapping their new four-stroke engines in conventional GP chassis and bodywork, Honda had taken the chance to stand well back and examine afresh the task of getting a motorcycle around a racetrack as quickly as possible. That is why the machine all but dominated the inaugural MotoGP season, winning 14 of the year's 16 races. Yamaha were the only factory who came close, their M1 initially off the pace, but winning two of the last seven races after a major redesign.

Valentino's own record was similarly impressive, although his season was something of a game of two halves. He won all but one of the first nine races, yet won only three of the final seven. He took pole at all but one of the first eight races, but didn't take a single pole from the last eight, and indeed, he was on the second row more often than the first during the second half of the campaign. This wasn't so much to do with him easing his pace as the crown headed his way – by midseason his championship lead was a yawning 95 points – as with his rivals getting faster. Not only were Biaggi and Checa up to speed on their M1s, but HRC started doling out more RCVs. Kato parked his NSR500s in August, while surprise-of-the-year Barros was granted a V5 for the final four races.

Valentino made only one real mistake during the first half of the season and he made it early, during round two at Welkom. In baking African heat he and Ukawa finished almost half a minute ahead of the pack, Capirossi the only man anywhere near their pace and flirting with disaster at every corner. But Vale got everything wrong – bike settings, tyre choice and race strategy. No doubt about it – that day galvanised his attitude for the next half dozen or so races.

His first mistake was to reject the RCV's slipper clutch, designed to ease the four-stroke's engine braking into turns. 'I was still trying to understand the four-stroke and there was too much to think about. I didn't understand the slipper system, so I wanted to use a normal clutch. We tried the slipper clutch in practice at Suzuka and Welkom but I preferred to race with the standard clutch, but after my mistake on the last lap at Welkom, JB said I must race with the slipper clutch at Jerez. The bike was not stopping well at Welkom, that's why we lost the race.'

That was one reason, anyway. Valentino had also chosen a softer rear tyre than Ukawa, expecting that he would be able to run away out front and ease his pace in the final laps. The third element of his downfall was his tactics: during the race he couldn't shake off his team-mate who then struck home his advantages on the final lap, using a harder Michelin and the slipper clutch that gave him much-improved corner-entry control.

The result was reminiscent of Doohan's three 'tow truck' defeats of 1996 and '97 when the great Aussie was beaten by Repsol Honda team-mates Alex Criville and Tady Okada who doggedly stuck to his tailpipes, then skidded past on the final lap. Doohan reserved his deepest scorn for these tactics and communicated his feelings with a look of thunder while standing on the podium. For now, Valentino just kept on grinning.

He could afford to. With the slipper clutch fitted, he was back to his winning ways at Jerez, two seconds ahead of NSR-mounted Kato, and at Le Mans, where he won a rain-shortened race by just two tenths from Ukawa. He even stayed on board to win at Mugello – his first home-race finish since '99, and therefore his first premier-class victory on Italian tarmac, 2.4 seconds ahead of Biaggi. The fans went nuts, thronging onto the track in their thousands and scaring the hell out of riders on their slowdown lap. As they headed into turn one at over 120mph, riders were confronted by a wall of wandering punters and it was a miracle that no one was hurt or killed in the mayhem. At Catalunya, he headed home Ukawa once more, using his favourite tactic – running with the leading pack until the closing stages, then letting it all hang out.

It looked easy, but it wasn't. The RCV was less precarious to ride than the old two-stroke but somehow this made life harder for Valentino, not easier. 'Is strange because the four-stroke's sweeter power delivery makes it easier out of corners but that makes it harder to make a difference against other guys at the end of a race. The 500's power was more wild, so the bike was more difficult to ride, but if you took risks in the final laps and you made two or three "spins", you could make the difference against the others. It's not impossible to do that with this bike, just more difficult.'

The RCV was also faster, more powerful and heavier than the 500, and therefore physically more demanding; Valentino's face often betraying real exhaustion after races. 'The four-stroke is like a tractor to change direction! So I've had to ask Dainese to add extra padding in the palms of my gloves, because my hands were getting destroyed.'

The bike's extra mass was most noticeable at Assen, where an inspired Barros harried Valentino throughout, the lighter NSR so much more manoeuvrable through the track's high-speed direction changes. 'Barros was taking one second from me in the section where you have to change direction at 145mph. I wasn't sure I could beat him. When he arrive, he arrive from another planet, he go so fast. It's very difficult to use 100 per cent of the four-stroke at Assen, but I learned from him and he pushed my limit forward.' Once again, Vale held fire until Barros's tyres were past their best, then he pushed home his attack for a fifth successive win.

By Donington – amazingly enough his 100th GP – MotoGP was becoming all-too predictable. Until Friday morning, at least, when all hell broke loose in the Repsol pit. Ukawa tumbled big style as he attacked the treacherous and high-speed Craner curves on his very first lap, while Valentino jumped off at the much slower final hairpin moments later.

Both men were injured – badly beaten-up Ukawa out for the weekend, a groggy Vale carted off to hospital with concussion and a cracked left thumb. He was back the next day, demoralising his rivals by sauntering to pole and then backing that with another win after Checa had tumbled out of the lead.

If aching bones and a throbbing head couldn't beat him, what could? Germany's tortuous Sachsenring, perhaps, where he had slumped to his worst result of 2001. Qualifying certainly suggested that this wouldn't be his weekend. Sixth fastest for his first start of 2002 off the front row, this surely would be where the so far out-paced two-strokes would have their day. Jacque took pole on his YZR500 and looked favourite for the win until Barros took him out trying a pass that the most reckless of teenagers would have considered over optimistic. As the two 500s skittered across the tarmac, Valentino tip-toed past to take his sixth win in a row.

It seemed like nothing could stop him now. So he and some mates checked into Ibiza for the summer break, partying so hard that Vale's mind seemed elsewhere when the GP circus reconvened at Brno in late August. This turned out to be the RCV's first-ever defeat, although the Ibiza hangover wasn't to blame. Biaggi's M1 was bang on the pace now and Kato was on his own RCV for the first time. The trio ran away out front, the Yamaha ahead most of the way, Valentino struggling to find a way past. Then suddenly, he was in trouble and heading back to the pits so his crew could replace a chunked rear Michelin. He got going again but soon retired when he realised he was well out of the points.

So, what had gone wrong? Everyone already knew that the RCV was harder on its tyres than the other four-strokes, but this wasn't a problem until Yamaha had got the M1 sorted, forcing the RCV closer to its limits. Obviously, Valentino had burned his rear tyre as he fought with Biaggi and Kato. Or had he? In fact, HRC worked out that the RCV's slipper clutch was partly to blame. JB explains: 'The slipper clutch rides up the ramp, spreads the plates and slips. But when it gets really hot, the clearances change, so instead of, say, 0.1mm clearance for the slippage, there's less, so the clutch doesn't spread, which is why it sometimes doesn't work.' And therefore places extra stresses on the rear tyre.

Despite the Brno DNF, Valentino was still cruising the championship, and the next two races at Estoril and Rio proved that Lady Luck hadn't deserted him, she'd just taken a brief vacation. He won both races on flooded tracks, after Gibernau had crashed out of the lead at Estoril and Checa came off at Rio. This was four wins in a row inherited from riders sliding off just ahead of him. As they say in racing – to finish first, first you must finish.

He celebrated at Rio in fine style, abandoning his bike on the victory lap to join a bunch of friends he'd flown in from Tavullia for the occasion, all of them dressed in a special Brazil-style football strip. Valentino stood with them, holding aloft a replica of the football World Cup, a warming tribute to the GP's hosting nation, which had won the trophy for the fifth time earlier in the year. Later that night, Vale and his gang headed into Rio's hills to party, only to find their way blocked by security – gang warfare having erupted in the area, spoiling their fun.

So he was World Champion for the fourth time, at the age of just 23, and with four races to spare, no less. Not only that, but his 23rd premier-class race win had moved him ahead of legends like King Kenny Roberts, John Surtees and Geoff Duke in the all-time winners' list, and just a race or two behind Wayne Rainey and Kevin Schwantz. The legend was still growing, and yet this was where things started to get tough for Valentino.

When the MotoGP pack headed out of Europe for the three-race eastern tour – Japan, Malaysia and Australia on consecutive Sundays – HRC fulfilled its promise to equip Barros with a single RCV for the final four races of the season. The Brazilian veteran – who started his GP career back in 1986 after lying about his age to get a licence – climbed aboard the V5 for the first time on Friday morning at Motegi. He had already raced four-strokes on a handful of occasions during his career, winning the Suzuka Eight Hours in 1999, so the RCV's easygoing nature didn't come as a complete surprise, but the bike was even better than he had expected. By Sunday afternoon he was fast enough to inflict a shock defeat on Valentino, who got more desperate and more out of control as the race went on – his RCV well crossed-up into the turns and luridly sideways on the exits. By comparison, Barros was neat, tidy and in control. It would take JB a few more races to work out what had gone wrong.

Seven days later at Sepang, another defeat, this time after the race of the year – where Vale, Biaggi, Barros and Ukawa used the wide-open spaces of the huge Malaysian track to mug each other with no mercy. Fairing paint was exchanged during the race and a few harsh words after, Valentino being the worst behaved both on and off the track. Barros might well have won again if Vale hadn't thumped into him and sent them both way out wide, allowing Biaggi to escape from the chaos, chased to the flag by the three RCVs. An inspired final few laps got Valentino back into second, half a second down on the Yamaha, but he wasn't happy, accusing Ukawa of having had the impertinence to get in his way. (Presumably the phrase 'the pot calling the kettle black' doesn't exist in the Italian lexicon.) Barros's comment on the champ's mad move that may have cost the Brazilian the win was honest and straight to the point: 'It's all part of racing, I would've done the same to him.'

Two defeats in just one week had JB making deeper investigations into the main reason for Valentino's difficulties – the RCV's overstressed slipper clutch, or 'slippery clutch', as Vale endearingly calls it. A few days later at Phillip Island, he had the problem sussed. Back in August, HRC had equipped their RCVs with a new ram-air system that offered another five horses at peak revs (like they needed it), and it had taken JB and crew this long to work out that the set-up increased engine drag when going into turns. Valentino first raced the unit, featuring a revised fairing and airbox, to win at Estoril and Rio, where wet tracks had disguised the problems which came to light at the next two races. 'After those defeats we decided we needed to understand some more about the ram air,' says Burgess. 'So, at Phillip Island he tried one bike with the system and one without, and the one without felt better into corners. There's no real logical reason for it, except that the airbox still maintains some pressure even though the throttle is closed, which might make the engine-braking problem worse.'

Come Sunday, Barros was on fire again, taking off out front, Valentino the only guy able to run with him. With a few laps remaining the RCV upstart was pushed back to second, saving his best for a last-lap counter attack into Honda hairpin. And this time, it was Barros's slipper clutch that went AWOL, the black and white Honda flying up the slip road, narrowly avoiding a collision. This was Valentino's 11th win of the year and a landmark 50th GP win – one more and he would equal Doohan's record of 12 wins in one season.

The season finale at Valencia was Australia all over again – the fastest two RCV riders were inches apart and miles ahead of the pack, but the finishing positions reversed this time, Barros resisting a desperate final-lap assault from Valentino. Such was their pace that they blew apart the two-year-old 500 race record by 65 seconds, an astonishing improvement of two seconds a lap.

So he hadn't quite matched Doohan's 12 wins-in-a-year record but he did establish a new record for the most points scored in a season, bettering Doohan's 1997 campaign by 15, although only because there'd been one extra race in 2002. Nevertheless, this was a towering achievement, just like his forebear's five years previously. Vale had finished 15 of the 16 races and all of them in first or second place, just as the former champ had done in '97. It was enough for many onlookers to pronounce him not just one of the greatest, but the greatest. And all this as he was hanging up his leathers and climbing into a Nomex suit for his World Rally debut just two weeks later.

The Rally of Great Britain, staged mostly along narrow, greasy forest trails in South Wales, wasn't the easiest way to enter the sport, and his much-hyped entry was one of the biggest stories of the event. But Valentino had plenty on his side – a factory Peugeot 206 (Honda weren't too happy about this), backing from Michelin, an experienced co-driver and some serious intent although he was setting his sights low. 'The main goal is to have fun,' he said during preparations, 'and to have fun I think the most important thing is to arrive at the end, or nearly the end, or anyway, don't make a mistake at the beginning because I like very much to drive the car.' Too bad, he lasted less than 12 miles before launching the 206 into a ditch. Disgusted at his mistake, Vale slunk away from the scene of the crime, hitching a lift back to London with dad, leaving reporters' questions unanswered. It seemed that he wasn't quite ready to desert bikes and take up a full-time four-wheel career.

The rally disaster was the worst thing that had happened to him all year, but at least he could now look forward to a bit of peace and quiet before Christmas. Fat chance. A fortnight before the holidays, Valentino was forced into hiding for fear of his life. His name had been attached to letter bombs sent to several European corporations by an anarchists group called the Five Cs (from the Spanish translation of its name: 'Unit against jails, capitalism, prison officers and cells'), a well-established organisation with a reputation for extreme violence. It was the Repsol link that moved him into the line of fire. 'I stay most of the time in London and when I go to Italy I have the police with me, but is not a big problem, the journalists make bigger.' And, typically, he found a silver lining to this dark cloud. 'From one point of view is not so bad, because I don't have to go to some boring events or so many boring press interviews. Maybe I write the letter of threat myself next year!'

Not the best end to what had been his greatest-ever season. But 2003 was to hold many new challenges, most interestingly, Biaggi's return to Honda power. Valentino knew exactly what to expect from his long-time rival, who had ended 2002 second overall after an impressive late-season surge. 'For sure it will be fun to have both of us on the same bike. We've raced together since 2000, all the times with different bikes, and all the time he says I win because I have a

Honda. The problem is that Biaggi always has an answer, so if he arrives behind me next year it will be because I have a factory bike, just like he was with Doohan during the 1998 season.' But Valentino would have more to worry about than Mad Max in 2003 ...

Chapter 8

THE MAN WITH TWO BRAINS

Vale bought himself an early birthday present in January 2003 – a big house in Ibiza. Well, you could argue that he had earned it. And the four-times World Champion chose his hideaway well, in accordance with the estate agent's maxim: location, location, location, or in this case: party, party, party.

Ibiza has been Europe's party island for years, and not merely since the late 1980s, when it played host to the pills, thrills and bellyaches of the first Ecstasy generation. Situated about 70 miles off Spain's Mediterranean coast, the smallest of the Balearic islands became a sanctuary for Spanish artists, gays and assorted liberals and hedonists during the years of General Franco's fascist dictatorship. During the late Sixties, hippies began to populate the island, then the emerging jet set, and in the late Seventies GP racing's new glamour stars used to holiday in the Ibizan palace of a top Spanish GP rider, tracing out the world's racetracks in cocaine: 'Okay, you do the hairpin, I do the main straight ...'

In these more sober days of professional sport, Ibiza at least gives Valentino a chance to have some fun away from the glaring eyes of the Italian media. He had decided to buy his own Ibizan lair after a large holiday on the island the previous August. 'Very much happen on that holiday, maybe too much ...' he said ruefully, revealing a growing love of all-night party chaos. But then Vale has never been one for early nights, nor does he have an obsessively anal attitude to training, an approach endorsed by 1976 and '77 500 champ Barry Sheene, who died of cancer just weeks before the 2003 season got underway. 'Barry say is not important for you go to bed at

10pm or get up early to go to the gym – the most important is to give 100 per cent when necessary.' Too right, mate.

Of course, with the late nights came the girls, and Valentino was getting through them at a rate. One of the few big-name riders to count himself 'single', he had finally copped onto the fact that he is young, rich and the ladies love him, so why on earth would he want to go steady just yet? As Italian MotoGP mover and shaker Carlo Pernat says: 'I've never seen so many girls around a rider, maybe Barry Sheene or Marco Lucchinelli (500 World Champ in 1981) but never so many. Valentino doesn't like to stay with a girl more than two or three months. He still lives like a kid now, with the same friends, the same way of life. After the racing is finished it's impossible to find him, no one knows where he goes, maybe he's in London, maybe he's in a disco with some friends he's known since he was a boy. He never changes, he doesn't want to be famous, he doesn't want a movie star girlfriend, he doesn't want to be in the papers with famous people.'

Valentino excuses himself by insisting that long-term girlfriends don't fit the GP lifestyle. 'I brought a girlfriend to the Barcelona race but now is finished,' he said midway through 2003. 'When you make this life is very difficult to have a girl. If you bring her to a GP maybe she's bored, so I stay alone at races, is better. Then when you stay one week at a racetrack, you come back home and you have some power to use, you need to have fun, go out with friends, go to the disco, but your girlfriend has just stayed one week doing all this kind of stuff, so when I come home, she say "can we see a movie?" So is difficult.'

It wasn't just the girls who distracted him in 2003: the Italian media gave him a particularly tough time over a midseason slump in results, gruelling negotiations for a third HRC contract dragged on for much of the summer, and his fame was still growing, along with MotoGP itself. The latest four-strokes were faster and noisier than the previous year's, so GP bikes had become what they always should have been – too fast, too loud, too insane – and finally people were getting turned on to MotoGP. The 2003 MotoGP paddock was one big feeding frenzy, the whiff of serious money everywhere and, of course, Valentino was still the 'face of the sport', as well as its global ambassador, charming fans wherever he went, fronting Dorna's pre-event press conferences at all 16 races.

So was it all about to get too much? 'It feels a little bit like I carry everything – I do every Dorna conference since Suzuka 2001, but this is only because the points leader must always do this job. Maybe I should change my tactic – slow at the start of the season, but take first position at the end! Now is also very difficult with all the fans in the paddock. A few years ago it wasn't like this. If I went out of my motorhome I sign some autographs, now is impossible to be outside my motorhome because I can't go anywhere. I feel like I have no time to think about riding the bike, so maybe my riding suffer. And, of course, some Italian journalists give me a hard time. Now if I win is normal, but if I don't win is a disaster, big headlines everywhere. This is difficult for the concentration, but this is the work of a rider; a very good rider must have two brains – one for all the problems away from the track, the other for all the problems on the track. If you can't cut your head into two parts, is better you get another job.'

So was he ready to jack it all in for another job, or maybe just retire and become a hippy, like dad? After all, he already had a few mill in the bank, and he's not the kind of guy who needs Lear jets or helicopters to boost his ego. 'No, I'm still young, so when I wake up and have nothing to do, is like fack, is very bad. It's too early to stop, not because of money but only because I love to ride the bike, is a shame that you have to do all the other shit, but that's the price to ride the best bike in the world.'

And the RCV was still the best bike in the world, but only just. Ducati entered MotoGP in 2003 with its first GP bike in three decades – the 240hp Desmosedici V4. The Bologna factory had often beaten Honda in World Superbike and their new V4 was breathtakingly fast straight out of the box. Ducati had winning riders as well – its own former Supers champ Troy Bayliss and Loris Capirossi. They were both lightning quick from the get-go, Capirossi topping the pre-season tests at Catalunya that Valentino had ruled the previous March. Suzuki also had an all-new bike, while Aprilia, Yamaha and Kawasaki had been working hard on their four-strokes. But most significantly, Honda had expanded its RCV line-up to seven riders, American Superbike champ Nicky Hayden joining Vale at Repsol Honda, Ukawa switching to Sito Pons's Camel-backed outfit where he partnered Biaggi, Kato joining Sete Gibernau at Telefonica Honda and Japanese Superbike firebrand Makoto Tamada all on his own at Pramac Honda.

Valentino knew what this meant – a much tougher season. 'It will be important to always arrive on the podium at every race and to be consistent,' he said before the Japanese GP. In fact Suzuka proved to be a bit of a pushover. Capirossi stunned onlookers by leaping into the lead from the fourth row – the Duke the fastest bike on the straights – until the sweeter-handling RCVs took over, Vale defeating Biaggi by an emphatic six seconds. During 2002, he had not beaten anyone by more than 2.5 seconds in the dry: perhaps this wasn't going to be so difficult after all.

Sadly, Suzuka 2003 won't be remembered for the result; it will go down in history as the race that did for HRC's favourite son Kato. The little Japanese died from injuries received in a horrific race accident that triggered a new and anxious debate about safety. The reasons for Kato's crash remain hazy, but riders were united in their condemnation of Suzuka, claiming that the epic figure-of-eight circuit, built way back in 1961, was too dangerous for 200mph motorcycles. 'The four-strokes are very, very fast,' said Vale. 'And they're heavier so they're difficult to stop, so we need more run-off area, more than at Suzuka.' The immediate upshot, apart from placing Suzuka's GP future in jeopardy, was the formation of a riders' safety council that would mostly involve Valentino, Gibernau, Suzuki's Kenny Roberts Junior and Proton rider Nobuatsu Aoki. The four riders would tour each circuit, advising about the requirements for safety improvements, both immediate and long term.

Having never regained consciousness, Kato died two weeks after the accident. Valentino was in London when he heard the news from Juan Martinez, his 2002 Showa suspension technician who, significantly as it would turn out, had defected to Gibernau's crew for the new season. Months later, Vale could only talk of Kato's death with a kind of saddened anger, like he didn't want to talk about it, like he hadn't yet dealt with it. That's what racers do – they're in denial about the worst thing that can happen. Only Aprilia's new MotoGP signing, Colin Edwards seemed capable of confronting the reality. 'This is the ultimate price you pay for living the dream,' said the reigning Superbike champ.

Days after Kato had passed away, the GP circus reconvened in South Africa for round two, the paddock mostly suffering a kind of shellshock. It was hardest for the younger members of the scene, who had never experienced this kind of thing, for it had been a decade since the last GP death. Kato's favoured number 74 was everywhere at Welkom – on riders' helmets, on their leathers, on the bikes, on the pit walls, on fans' tributes – and most certainly in team-mate Gibernau's heart. The Spaniard added some fairytale to the nightmare by taking pole position and victory, defeating Vale in a nail-biting final few laps. But those who suggested that the champ had allowed him to win were straying well into fantasy. In fact

Valentino had mucked up again, like he had at Welkom '02, except this time his mistake was the reverse of the previous year's.

In 2002, he had chosen a too-soft rear tyre for the demanding Welkom circuit, but this time he over-compensated for that error by choosing a too-hard rear. He knew the tyre would take a while to come good, but he reckoned he'd have grip when he most needed it – at the end. But the tyre took too long to come in and on his way to the front he got stuck into a long-running melee with up-for-a-fight rookie Bayliss. The final few laps were a classic: Valentino biting into Gibernau's lead at every turn, but 0.3 seconds adrift at the flag. 'It seemed like Kato was with Sete today,' he said. 'He had his own aggression with Daijiro's precision.'

And precision wasn't all that Gibernau inherited from the late former 250 champ. Once the European sector of the championship was underway the 30-year-old had Kato's factory RCVs at his disposal. In 2003 there were two kinds of RCV – customer bikes leased to satellite-team riders Gibernau, Biaggi and Tamada, and full-factory bikes ridden by official HRC men Rossi, Kato, Hayden and Ukawa. The difference wasn't vast, as Gibernau had demonstrated at Welkom in his last customer-bike race, a point largely lost on Biaggi who would continue whingeing and moaning about his customer bikes. But a difference there was, which the maturing Gibernau would soon put to the best of use.

Not quite yet though – Valentino won again at Jerez, his second victory in a topsy-turvy run of win one race, lose the next that would continue until things went awry midseason. Two weeks later at rainy Le Mans, Gibernau won again by a hair's breadth, MotoGP's newest star always happy to take bigger risks than most, especially in tricky wet/dry conditions. The pair were side by side into the last turn, both of them running off the track as Gibernau stole the quickest line to the chequered flag. At Mugello the status quo was restored, Valentino riding his heart out to win ahead of Capirossi's astonishingly fast Ducati that touched 206mph on the main straight.

At this stage in 2002 he had led the series by a gaping 43 points, but this year he was still 32 points ahead despite two defeats. Things appeared to be going according to plan, but Valentino was about to go into a bit of a wobble. During June and July he went four races without a win, the Italian media hysterically proclaiming his demise as MotoGP's main force. As everyone knows, the media's whole modus operandi is based upon the premise of building people up to knock 'em down. That way publishers sell twice as many newspapers – by getting the public excited by new faces, then by rubbing those faces in the dirt. Rossi was in crisis, the Italian press ranted, he'd become so obsessed with money during his contract negotiations that he'd forgotten how to ride. The hacks had a point – Valentino hadn't gone so long without a win since his debut 500 season in 2000. During his first premier title-winning years (2001 and 2002) he never went more than two races without a winner's gong.

So what was wrong with the Doctor? Was he really blinded by the dollar signs, was he getting lazy, or was it something deeper than that? First, we should take a look at the four GPs that defeated him: Catalunya, Assen, Donington and Sachsenring. He made three mistakes in those four races. At Catalunya he ran off the track after nearly colliding with Capirossi, at Donington he won the race but was docked ten seconds because he'd passed Capirossi under yellow flags (gifting the win to Biaggi) and at Sachsenring he mucked up the final turn while disputing the lead with Gibernau. He made no such gaff at Assen, where he rode to a cautious third in dangerously wet conditions, Gibernau once again the risk taker and brave winner.

Valentino happily fronted up to his three mistakes. 'At Catalunya I am under the screen and when I look up all I see is Ducati. I think Loris brake early, but is my mistake, like on the street, is the guy behind who mustn't hit the guy in front.' No biggie then. Donington was even more straightforward – anyone can miss a yellow flag waved 50 metres away – while Sachsenring was undoubtedly the most interesting of Vale's errors. During the early stages of the race he built an apparently comfy 2.5 second lead over Gibernau, but then let that advantage evaporate, allowing his rival ahead, preferring to delay his winning move to the final lap. This was pure laziness – letting those 2.5 seconds go – followed by cockiness and too much tactics, thinking he could leave it until the penultimate corner. 'My mistake was to consider Sete less dangerous than he is. With Biaggi I always give more because he's a better rider.' Rossi's last-lap plan left him no second chance, whereas Gibernau's non-plan worked perfectly, the Spaniard beating Vale at the very last corner. 'I had no plan,' affirmed Gibernau. 'Because when you have a plan and it doesn't work, you're in trouble.'

Vale knew he had to win at Brno if he was to avert another media onslaught. The previous August when he arrived in the Czech Republic he'd already won eight of the first nine races, this time he had won just three, so there would be no mercy from the Italian press if he messed up again. Which he didn't – Valentino had learned from his blunders to win Brno, beating Gibernau at the end of a thrilling race that had also involved Bayliss and Capirossi. 'After my stupid mistakes, just from thinking too much, I change my tactics: ride 100 per cent and if anyone come past, attack immediately!'

Valentino's laziness/over-confidence/tactical over-load was nothing new in top-level racing. You only need go back to Mick Doohan to recognise a similar pattern during The Mighty One's years of dominance. In 1995 and '96 Doohan made several cock-ups that allowed lesser-lights Darryl Beattie and Alex Criville to beat him. The root of those mistakes was a lack of focus brought on by a dearth of opposition that might truly stretch him. Likewise, Rossi had reached a point where he was feeling unchallenged by his peers. 'You always need to stay determined and motivated,' he says. 'When the fight is good, is no problem to find motivation, but if the racing is too easy, is difficult to stay concentrated.' Life had been getting too easy, and when life gets too easy, it has a habit of suddenly becoming rather difficult. But the great thing is that those defeats never really bothered him: 'When Mick arrive second is a disaster for him, but I'm a bit different, for me is more important to have fun.'

And there were further similarities between Rossi's 2003 experience and Doohan's own reign. As Honda number ones, both men got to ride the best bikes and develop them, only for their hard-won set-up secrets to be distributed amongst other Honda riders. This used to drive Doohan crazy, although Valentino was more sanguine about it. 'The Honda is the best bike and once you make the basic setting, is quite easy to ride. Now all the Honda riders have my data from last year, especially Sete who now has Juan (Martinez) as his chief mechanic. Juan was my suspension technician last year, so he knows my way of working, so is very easy for him to arrive at the track and fix the bike, which makes it more easy for Sete.'

So great was his relief at Brno – his first win in five races – that he was back to his joking ways on the podium. We'd not seen such frolics for some while – the pressures of racing in the MotoGP class may have sucked the fun out of him but here was proof that he could still be a happy-go-lucky youngster when he felt like it. This time he was just too happy not to do something daft, so he wore a prison inmate's hat and ball and chain to poke fun at the Italian media, joining some similarly attired mates to smash some boulders with pickaxes and sledgehammers. 'They said I was in crisis because I'd been beaten at the last four races,' he said. 'Leading the championship and finishing on the podium obviously isn't enough for them, so now I must work on the chain gang!'

And beneath the striped cap was a new red hairdo. 'I saw a girl on the beach in Ibiza last week with the same hair, it looked cool, so I went for the same,' he said, denying that the colour had anything to do with a rumoured move to Ducati. The Rossi-to-Ducati story had been grabbing headlines all summer, Vale happily fanning the flames by remarking that it'd be 'a dream' to ride for the Italian brand. At first the story seemed little more than that – mere silly season bullshit that Valentino might employ to his advantage to pump up the dollars. 'When you decide a contract, money is maybe fourth or fifth place, is not your number-one target,' he said at Brno. 'Before money you need to decide if you want to ride that bike, if you want to work with those men and that team. Then you decide the money.' Valentino's insistence that this wasn't just about the dollars drew hoots of derision from some corners of the paddock, but as the weeks passed it became obvious that the Honda talks were indeed going seriously wrong. By Portugal the negotiations were starting to get properly complicated as Yamaha hinted that they were also chasing the champ's signature. Now those two brains would come in real handy …

On track at Estoril he beat Biaggi by a comfy two seconds, completing a hat trick of wins at Rio with a three-second victory over Gibernau. Perhaps he wasn't past his sell-by date after all. In fact Valentino's next few races would prove the exact opposite: he was riding better than ever. Every race told the same story – check me out, this is what I'm worth – and the more Yamaha saw, the more they knew they had to have him. Five and a half million pounds (plus the offer of a £3 million title bonus) is a lot of cash, but when it makes the difference between winning and losing in biking's biggest race series, it's nothing.

As the MotoGP circus embarked on its annual odyssey to Motegi, Sepang and Phillip Island, Valentino admitted that the Honda talks were on the verge of breakdown. 'Dealing with HRC is impossible,' he said. He may not have been exaggerating. HRC's all-consuming MotoGP domination was undoubtedly having an effect on some of the company's higher-ranking staff, like managing director and wannabe samurai warlord Kohji Nakajima who was now swaggering around the paddock like he owned the place. Which he kind of did.

Following Ducati's wake-up call at Catalunya, HRC had raised the stakes with its V5, a few software and hardware modifications accelerating the bike well ahead of the opposition. At Rio and Motegi the first five machines over the finishing line were all RCVs, the factory's most dominant display since the start of the new four-stroke era.

But the fact that Honda had far and away the best MotoGP machine wasn't looking like it was going to be enough to keep Valentino. Perversely the RCV's obvious superiority was driving him in the opposite direction. Not only was he finding HRC's attitude distasteful, he had also discovered that he couldn't win with the Italian media – if he lost races, he was so over, but if he won them it was only because he had the fastest motorcycle. There were two potential solutions to this particular dilemma – ignore the media's never-ending bleatings or swap factories.

While admitting that it would be 'an adventure' to go with Yamaha, Vale continued his talks with HRC. New contracts were formulated, presented, rejected, modified, presented

Right: 'You calling me a chicken?' Valentino and friend celebrate at Catalunya '98, scene of the third of his 14 250 wins. (Gold & Goose)

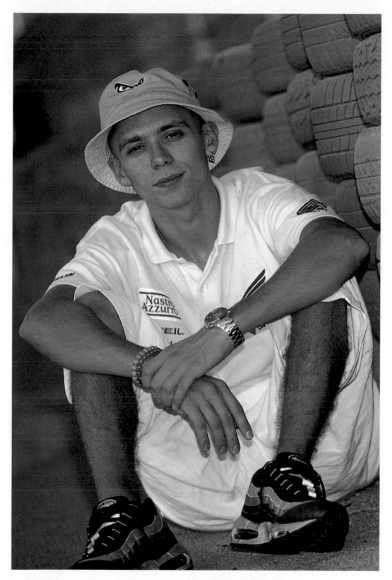

Left: *Defeating boredom between practice sessions at the Sachsenring.* (Milagro)

Above: *Valentino has done a bit of growing up over the past few years, revealing a more contemplative side.* (Gold & Goose)

Left: *On a hot lap during qualifying, Mugello 2001.* (Gold & Goose)
Above: *'Yup, thanks Honda, you've been great.'* (Milagro)

once again and once more rejected as he worked his way around the Far East. At Sepang he wrapped up the title with another untroubled win over Gibernau and Biaggi, then a few hours later he was spotted in the far corner of the darkened paddock carpark, deep in discussion with two Yamaha mechanics. And there were giveaways from within his pit, his faithful crew asking paddock colleagues 'what are Yamaha like to work for?' Because if he did make the move, Vale wanted JB & Co to go with him.

Some insiders reckoned that he had already signed with Yamaha and would make an announcement at the following weekend's Australian GP, now that the title was safely tucked away. Valentino did make an announcement Down Under, but it wasn't the one people had expected.

The Phillip Island race was possibly the greatest of his career, eclipsing even his win from the third row of the grid at Donington in 2001 and announcing his genius to Honda, Yamaha and the rest of the world. Of course, everyone expected Rossi to win, even though the spectacularly fast seaside circuit has a deserved reputation for providing scarily close and unpredictable racing. No, his 58th career victory wasn't the surprise, it was the manner in which he achieved it that was utterly remarkable. Involved in an intense skirmish for the lead with team-mate Nicky Hayden and Yamaha's Marco Melandri, Vale copped a ten-second penalty for overtaking while yellow flags were displayed where Bayliss had crashed.

This was the same punishment he'd been given at the British GP three months earlier but with one significant difference: at Donington he only learned of the penalty after the race was over, too late to do anything about it, but this time his pit signals informed him of the situation shortly after he had taken the lead. 'When I first saw "minus ten" on my board I didn't understand what it meant. Then the board told me "P8" and I said to myself "Fack, what happened?" Like Donington, I never saw any yellow flag. But once I understood my board I decided to fight very hard to beat the ten-second penalty. I had already won the championship, so there was nothing to lose.'

Now aware of the Herculean task that lay before him, Vale demolished the track record pretty much every lap, disappearing over the horizon to beat Capirossi by an astonishing 15.2 seconds and Hayden and the rest of the pack by more than 20 seconds. This was total demoralisation for his rivals who had been given a depressing hint of what he could do when he really needed to. And then he delivered this killer line at the post-race press conference: 'This was maybe the first time I rode a complete race at 100 per cent.' What?

Phillip Island also made Vale the fourth most successful premier-class racer in history, his 32nd big-bike win moving him ahead of eighties legend Eddie Lawson. Only Doohan, Mike Hailwood and Giacomo Agostini now stood ahead of him – statistical proof that he was up there with the greatest racing legends of all time.

But still no announcement. It almost seemed like he was enjoying the media hubbub, grinning from ear to ear as he watched the Italian journalists work themselves into a daily sweat over his future whereabouts. Having suffered at their hands during the summer, the refusal to announce his 2004 plans was like some kind of sweet revenge: no one had ever seen the Italian media work so hard.

Of course, JB had some thoughts on his rider's future plans, suggesting that Yamaha had plenty of work to do if they wanted Valentino to bring home biking's premier crown. 'It would be good to know what Yamaha are planning for the future,' said JB. 'Because if they're planning to persevere with the bike they've got, they're kidding themselves.' Harsh words perhaps but Yamaha's engineers knew they needed to improve the M1 and that's another reason they seemed prepared to meet Vale's demands. Not only was Rossi the fastest rider in the world, he also has renowned development skills, something that Yamaha had lacked ever since its most recent 500 champ Wayne Rainey crashed out of racing in September 1993.

The season finale at Valencia turned out to be another Rossi romp – his ninth pole of the year, his ninth win of the year and another lap record at the only GP track at which he'd never won a race. Once again he beat Gibernau at a canter, then readied himself for the press conference where the worst kept secret in MotoGP would be confirmed. 'It was around the time of Sepang that we started to think about this change,' he said. 'I have done everything with the Honda – win in the dry and the rain, win at my best track and at my worst track – so I feel I have finished my work with this bike. I've had an incredible four years with Honda – three World Championships and 33 wins from 64 races. Maybe my choice seems a little bit crazy, but we will see next year. Officially, I am still a Honda rider until 31 December, so I can't speak about other machines. But I have one last favour to ask Honda: that they will let me try my new bike before the end of the year!'

Of course, Honda refused. Now the factory was acting like a jilted lover, and pretty soon Valentino was going to break its heart good and proper.

Chapter 9

AND NOW: MISSION IMPOSSIBLE

Joy has always been the heart and soul of Valentino's racing genius. He's out there doing what he loves, what he adores (while also mugging his rivals, then slicing them into small pieces, obviously). But during 2004 his riding displayed a new and fiercer aggression, fed by a little bitterness, some anger and a real lust for revenge. However politely he had taken his leave of Honda, Valentino was deeply unhappy with his old bosses, unhappy enough to have agreed to swap the best bike on the grid for an inferior machine, while not even taking a pay rise along the way. Can you imagine Michael Schumacher quitting Ferrari to drive for McLaren without doubling his fee? Or Ronaldo signing to Leicester City without a multi-million pay rise? Paddock rumours suggested that Rossi's primary contract earnings and bonuses may actually have dropped by a few per cent in 2004, though at around £8.5 million he was hardly struggling to pay the rent.

But this is Rossi. He's in racing for the buzz, for the fun, these are his motivating forces. Sure, he enjoys winning and earning shed loads of cash but if these were his fundamental inspirations he would never have moved to Yamaha, whose M1 was both slow and evil handling. While most other racers would've put up with HRC's aloofness to ensure they had the fastest bike on the track, Valentino simply couldn't bear it. But boy, was he going to make sure HRC paid for pissing him off. And if his own reward wasn't going to come from amassing more riches, it would come from inner satisfaction, from that warm glow that you might gain from giving your boss the finger, then proving he's dumber than he thinks he is and, most important of all, dumber than you are. This was the fuel for Vale's new aggression.

And it wasn't only Valentino who was seething. Jeremy Burgess and three of his faithful four-strong crew (Ansiau, Briggs and Coleman) followed their rider to Yamaha. JB and Briggs had both offered to stay where they were but HRC wouldn't agree to their terms, so in one fell swoop Honda had lost its best rider and its best pit crew. Bizarrely, it seems that there were some people at HRC who actually wanted Rossi to leave; how else could they have let go the best racer in the world, who also happens to be the best development rider and the most promotable motorcyclist on earth? The twisted logic goes like this – if Honda could win the world title without Rossi, it would prove once and for all that the company does indeed build the best motorcycles. In other words, the never-ending debate of man versus machine (which is more crucial?) was about to answered.

Of course, there were other factors in Valentino's defection from Honda to Yamaha. He wasn't just pissed off with HRC, he also fancied a new challenge, mindful of the mid-2003 slump brought on by having life too easy on Honda's RCV. Valentino likes to climb mountains. Why? Because they're there, because they make life more interesting for young, thrusting males. So however grimly determined he was to avenge Honda, Valentino also found that the move to Yamaha brought with it a breath of fresh air. 'I knew that if I could win on the Yamaha it would bring me great joy,' he says. 'That thought overcame any fears and doubts I'd had about making the move.'

Burgess was also delighted with his own decision to join his adopted son, quitting Honda after 20 years and a bunch of premier-class crowns. 'I feel euphoric,' he said during the first weeks of 2004. 'I'd had a comfortable time at Honda, I'd won three titles with Valentino, five with Mick (Doohan), so I knew what it was like rolling through five, one after the other, and we were going through that again. It wasn't Honda's fault that it was boring, but it was like that to me.'

So here was Rossi's merry band of thrill seekers, striking out on some quixotic adventure that had as much chance of going pear-shaped as turning into a swashbuckling fairytale. They were joining Yamaha's oft-criticised M1 project (M1 officially stands for Mission One but cynics were already calling it Mission Impossible), to take on the RCV hordes led by factory Repsol riders Alex Barros (replacing Valentino) and Nicky Hayden, plus satellite teamsters Max Biaggi, Sete Gibernau and co. Now, Valentino and his crew would never have signed up for this mission if they'd been that scared of losing, which is another mark of a true sportsman – stick your balls on the line and go for it, and if it doesn't work out, at least you know you had a go. That's not the kind of thing you see much of these days …

But before the brave quest could begin, Valentino had some serious waiting to do. HRC had churlishly refused to grant him an early release him from his contract, so he would have to wait to ride the M1 until the new year. And it was worse than that. Newly introduced MotoGP regulations had imposed a one-month moratorium on testing from mid-December to give overworked teams some chance of a proper winter break. Normally Valentino would've been delighted at being told to go on holiday but not this year. Instead of commencing testing immediately after the season-ending Valencia GP (as most of his rivals had done) he had to sit it out until mid-January, leaving him less than three months to knock the badly under-achieving M1 into shape. That made up everyone's mind – there was no way Rossi was going to achieve success during the first year of his two-year deal with Yamaha. Even Valentino predicted he'd only be second or third in 2004. 'When I moved to Yamaha the target was always to put the M1 on top, but I had a two-year plan to solve the bike's problems and then take it to the top.' Remember, the Yamaha had not even won a single race since October 2002.

His first date with the Yamaha was set for 24 January, at Sepang. Media interest in the test was unprecedented, so much so that Yamaha banned journalists from the pits area. They wanted Rossi and JB left to work alone – though not quite alone. Yamaha had dozens and dozens of engineers on site to listen to every word spoken by the pair.

Apprehensive before his first handful of laps on the M1, Valentino found the bike less of a disaster than the doomsayers had suggested. 'But I immediately understood that racing would be more difficult with the Yamaha compared to the Honda,' he said. Nevertheless his pace was stunning on the first day – 1.1 seconds inside his own lap record and just one or two tenths slower than Max Biaggi and Sete Gibernau had managed during HRC's first tests of the year a few days earlier. Suddenly the mountain didn't look so tall after all.

But on the other hand maybe it did. When Yamaha and Honda shared Sepang for further tests a few weeks later, the RCVs had taken a leap forward. Valentino ended the session fifth quickest, behind Hayden, Biaggi, Gibernau and Colin Edwards, back at Honda after a miserable 2003 with Aprilia. And the next week at Phillip Island he was again fifth fastest. Valentino seemed only mildly rattled, pleading with Yamaha for more horsepower. And yet Yamaha's engineers were hardly being idle. They had already created three new prototype engines, with different firing intervals and cylinder heads, which Rossi had evaluated during the first two test sessions. Valentino immediately knew which motor he preferred – a brand-new unit with four-valve heads (instead of Yamaha's signature five-valve heads) and revised firing intervals (which gave it a gruff exhaust note, hence the nickname 'growler'). 'I like this engine because the power is more sweet, so it is more easy to ride,' he said. Only one problem: this engine was also the least powerful.

In mid-March at the Catalunya season prologue event, where all 2004 teams gathered for the first time, the Yamaha was more than 6mph down on the fastest bike, Loris Capirossi's Ducati, which achieved a jaw-dropping 216mph. Now, six miles an hour may not sound that much at over 200mph but it is a big difference, like standing still while someone jogs past you. Rossi wasn't standing still, however, he was riding harder than ever before, digging deeper into his gold mine of talent to compensate for the M1's obvious lack of straight-line speed. And it showed. The Catalunya weekend ended with an officially timed session, the prelude to the season-opening South African GP to be held a few weeks later. In treacherous, chilly conditions Valentino outpaced everyone, just as he'd done a year before on his RCV, then wasted no time in having a pop at his old bosses. 'It wasn't right that Honda said the bike is the most important thing, that wasn't fair on me or their other riders.' Rossi one, Honda nil. Man one, machine nil.

Of course, riding one quick lap isn't everything. The conventional wisdom before the South African GP went thus: Valentino may be able to outpace everyone while his tyres have enough grip to accommodate his awesome skills but what would happen over full race distance when he wouldn't have that traction? Even the man himself admitted that the bike only felt really good on super-sticky qualifying tyres, used for one or two flat-out laps in qualifying. So it didn't necessarily mean much when he topped Friday morning practice at Welkom and then beat Gibernau and Biaggi to pole position on Saturday afternoon. 'This is a bit of surprise!' he grinned, hardly able to contain his delight. 'And this pole position is worth ten with Honda.' It was already obvious that Valentino was enjoying his new job and getting on well with his new bosses.

And they were getting on with Valentino too. Like HRC in 2000, Yamaha personnel could only gaze in awe at his data traces. 'He is the same out of every corner,' said one Yamaha engineer. 'He gives the throttle a little yank to get the tyre spinning, then he keeps it spinning, but only just, by modulating the throttle. This way he has more control than riders who don't keep the tyre spinning.'

The next day Valentino made history – the first man in 55 years of GP racing to win back-to-back premier-class races on different makes of machinery. And the race was a thriller, a straight duel to the finish with long-time rival Biaggi, whose RCV was way quicker, threatening to gobble up the M1 every time the pair sped down Welkom's back straight. But Valentino was riding like an animal and hung on to win by just ten yards.

This was a breathtaking debut victory against massive odds, so improbable that not even Valentino had dared believe it was possible, which is why there were no zany victory celebrations, just him curling into a foetal ball and sobbing his little heart out; somehow he always seems to get the right mood for the moment. And then the inner glow: 'The next day I felt an enormous satisfaction because I had done what many people said couldn't be done. They said that Honda is unbeatable but I beat them at my first try!' Valentino was loving it – admitting that he derived huge pleasure from seeing crestfallen, chain-smoking HRC boss Kohji Nakajima wandering the Welkom paddock all alone after the race.

If the South African win had given Valentino a massive buzz and sent Yamaha staff into hysterics of joy, Burgess was typically more sanguine about the whole thing. From the word go he had refused to join in the transfer hubbub, despite his earlier criticism of the M1. 'The whole changing factories thing is all being blown out of proportion,' he said. 'To me it's just a change of tool: last year Valentino cut trees with a Makita, this year he's going in with a Stihl, I can't see what all the fuss is about.' Good old JB, you can always count on him to strip any situation of its glamour.

The M1 was certainly a different tool. It didn't have the RCV's brute force, it was a finer blade, made for someone brave, someone prepared to take risks and venture into places other riders wouldn't dare go. Which is why Valentino could win on the thing. Of course, the M1 had improved since JB had got his hands on it. Bringing his own tools – logic and pragmatism – to his new job, the Aussie had worked at maximising the M1's strengths rather than worrying about its weaknesses, so while Yamaha worked on engine stuff he focused on getting the most out of its sweet-handling chassis. He lengthened the M1's wheelbase to calm its snappy handling and raised the chassis to improve steering, while Michelin's new 16.5in tyre steadied the bike's dodgy front end. And Michelin had done its bit in other ways too. The French rubber gurus had introduced a wider rear slick during winter testing that allowed the Yamaha to exploit its corner-speed advantage. Some Honda riders even called this 16.5 rear 'the Yamaha tyre'. As Valentino said later in the year: 'If you have 10kmh less than the other guys, or five less horsepower, you can still win, but if you have worse tyres you are facked'.

Round two happened at Jerez, another track where corner speed counts for more than straight-line oomph, so Valentino was on pole again, edging out new Yamaha team-mate Carlos Checa and Gibernau. But race day dawned dark and grey, a spring downpour soaking the track. This was Valentino's first taste of the rain with the M1 and he didn't like it, surviving more than one out-of-the-seat moment to finish a distant fourth behind Gibernau, Biaggi and Barros, an ominous all-Honda podium.

But defeat in Spain wasn't a major worry. While JB had largely sorted the bike's dry-track behaviour he had to guess a wet set-up for Jerez which didn't give enough traction into or out of the turns. Things would surely be back to normal for round three at Le Mans. Except that they weren't. Yamaha may have furnished its favourite son with a slightly more powerful motor for the French GP but Valentino struggled with braking stability in the race, once again coming in fourth, and thus losing the championship lead to Gibernau, the Spaniard building momentum all the way.

Le Mans was Valentino's worst race in ages. In fact the whole day was a disaster: he slid off during morning warm-up (his first crash from the M1), he stalled the motor on the grid and then made a rare error during the race, removing a tear-off visor on the shortest of straights, which caused him to run wide at the next turn. That's what happens when you've got to ride over the edge to keep up, you start making silly mistakes ...

Or maybe he'd been distracted by something else. Before Le Mans Valentino had accepted an invitation from Ferrari to test Michael Schumacher's Ferrari F1 car. The brief but impressive outing triggered a flurry of reports that Vale would defect to F1 once his Yamaha contract expired at the end of 2005. 'I started my career in karts, the only reason I change to bikes is because the cost is too great, so why not race cars again?' he said. The Ferrari drive also pissed off most of his sponsors: Yamaha wasn't happy because the marque is part-owned by Ferrari's F1 rival Toyota, Gauloises seethed because Ferrari is backed by Marlboro and Michelin wasn't happy because Schumacher uses Bridgestones. But Valentino was doing the business on the M1, so they all had to swallow their pride and keep their mouths shut.

Schumi was present for the test and was impressed. 'Valentino was very good,' he said. 'I would say he could come into F1 at a certain level, which may be competitive, but to reach the final bit is usually difficult.' Then when Vale offered the most successful car racer in history a blast on his M1, Schumacher was just a little reticent. 'Going from two wheels to four is okay, going from four wheels to two isn't,' said Schumacher. Wimp.

If Valentino had messed up at Le Mans because he was trying too hard, he wasn't the only one pushing to new limits. JB and everyone else in project M1 were burning the midnight oil, toiling to find the correct settings to suit each new track. During his carefree Honda days, JB would sometimes be pouring himself a pint in the HRC hospitality tent by 5.30 on a Saturday evening. Now he wasn't getting to quench his thirst until 10 or 11 and his rider wasn't even ending up on the podium. Was the big adventure about to go awry?

If it was, Vale wasn't going to let this get to him. He turned up at Mugello two weeks later wearing a 'wooden' helmet, well, an AGV painted to look wooden, because in Italy fourth-place finishers are traditionally awarded a wooden spoon for their hopeless efforts. Perhaps this was a good time for some self-deprecation, since his chances at Mugello didn't seem so hot. The Italian track features GP racing's longest straight – a 1.1-mile nightmare for Yamaha. JB's advice was simple: 'It's a long straight here, Valentino, so keep your shoulders in and your toes up.' It wasn't all doom and gloom, however, because JB had fixed the braking stability problems that had done for Vale at Le Mans during a post-race test session at the French track. A few front fork adjustments and the M1 was a whole lot better.

Qualifying didn't go so well, Valentino only third, almost half a second down on pole-sitter and points leader Gibernau, who was getting proper support from HRC because he was now Honda's main title hope, ahead of struggling factory riders Barros and Hayden. The race was a total classic, in fact both Mugello races were mesmerising. During the first outing, stopped when rain began to fall after 19 laps, the lead changed 30 or so times as Valentino jousted with Gibernau, Biaggi and Makoto Tamada. The second race (run over just six laps, according to new MotoGP regulations) was even more thrilling, if only because conditions were so dangerous – a still damp track with a 210mph straight, and all the top guys on slick tyres. Yikes. After a few laps to suss the conditions, Valentino broke away to beat Gibernau by just three tenths, his ride earning this 'praise' from Aussie nutter Troy Bayliss: 'You have to hand it to Valentino, he puts it on the line, he was going like a maniac'.

The next Sunday at Catalunya Rossi beat Gibernau again, and once again a fortnight later at Assen, putting the pair equal on points. 'This was the key point in the championship,' he says. 'Sete was already in very good shape going into those three races but we were able to beat him anyway. That's when I began to think we could win the championship.' Valentino had scored a hat-trick of wins at three fast tracks where the Yamaha had been expected to struggle. But he was still riding on the absolute limit to stay ahead. At Assen he made a hard last-lap pass on Gibernau, then nearly fell at the next turn, colliding with the Spaniard's RCV. Gibernau was appalled by what he considered to be dirty riding and this was the beginning of the end of a beautiful relationship. For some years the pair had been good mates, getting pissed together on Sunday nights, going clubbing in Ibiza, but not any more.

Gibernau's hopes of getting his revenge the following weekend in Rio ended when he slid off on the second lap. And a few laps later Valentino was also down, the win going to first-time victor Tamada. Chastened by his first race tumble since Mugello 2001, Valentino struggled to fourth in the next race at the Sachsenring, his M1 bucking and weaving as he tried to bend it to his will. Meanwhile Biaggi won his first race of the year, heading another all-Honda podium and moving to within just one point of Rossi's series lead (while Gibernau slipped a few points behind after another tumble). It seemed that HRC was finally getting its act together because no matter how hard Valentino had ridden in Germany, he couldn't match the RCVs. HRC was firing new, go-faster parts at its favoured riders in reaction to Yamaha's success. And the M1 was still a strange beast. 'It is definitely a peculiar motorcycle – sometimes it tells me it likes a track, other times it tells me it hates a track. We have a fight every now and again but then we make up.'

And that's precisely what they did at Donington, Vale's happy hunting ground in the British Midlands. He took pole and won the race by two seconds, his easiest ride so far despite HRC's greatest efforts. 'HRC seem a little angry,' he grinned. 'They try so hard to kick my arse but they can't!' That British GP win eased him ahead in the title fight, now 12 points up on both Biaggi and Gibernau, which put him in good mood for MotoGP's summer break. As always, Valentino headed for Ibiza, where he had fun getting twisted at DC10, his favourite haunt of the moment. He also enjoyed some time in London, his affection for the British growing all the while. Looking out of the window of his Mayfair apartment one day, Valentino spotted a fat old man in another apartment block, stark-bollock naked and miming a tennis match. This kind of eccentric behaviour tickled the ex-pat racer: 'The English are raving mad, which is why I feel so comfortable living here.'

Back to business at Brno where HRC had more tune-up parts for Gibernau. He took a comfortable three second win over Vale, who couldn't match the RCV around this fast and wide track however hard he tried. Two weeks later in Portugal the pendulum swung again, the tortuous, bumpy Estoril track suiting Valentino so well that he scored his most emphatic victory so far, a couple of days after making the shock announcement that he would complete his two-wheel racing career with Yamaha. Some insiders suggested this meant something even more shocking – that he definitely would switch to F1 at the end of 2005, once he'd served his term with Yamaha. And you could see why he was looking around for new diversions. At Estoril his closest rival was Tamada, who finished a distant six seconds back, while Gibernau battled handling woes in fourth place. Biaggi's title hopes took a battering when he was taken out by Capirossi on the first lap.

HRC wasn't giving up yet, however. Next stop on the 16-race calendar was Motegi, the factory's own track which might almost have been built especially for the RCV. Motegi is all low-gear corners followed by long straights, the kind of place where the V5's awesome acceleration should be unbeatable. And not only that. HRC had an extra RCV on the grid, ridden by Tohru Ukawa, who'd retired from GPs at the end of 2003 to become a full-time test rider. Honda's plan was simple – pack the grid and make sure Rossi scores as few points as possible.

Honda was out of luck, however. Biaggi, Edwards and Hayden got taken out in a first turn pile-up that left Valentino out front and looking good. But he hadn't avoided the carnage by chance; he knows that Motegi's first corner is an accident black spot, so made damn sure he got into the turn in the safest place possible – first. Even so he didn't win the race. Unable to match Tamada's runaway pace he finished a distant second but that was good enough because Gibernau ended up way back in sixth, complaining of more chassis gremlins. So Rossi had come out of what should have been his toughest race of the year an extra ten points up on his biggest rival.

With four races to go he enjoyed a 39-point lead over the Spaniard; now it seemed there was no way he wasn't going to win the title.

The desert changed all that. For the first time in its history, GP racing was heading into the Middle East. Qatar's brand-new Losail track, built with oil and gas riches, was a money-no-object project – air-conditioned pits, massive run-off areas, the lot. But there was nothing the hosts could do to stop desert sand from getting onto the track. Unable to find decent grip during practice Valentino ran off the circuit at least eight times on Friday and Saturday. And then JB made the biggest mistake of his career. On the eve of race day Rossi's crew stole out onto the track aboard a scooter, found its rider's grid slot and performed a few burnouts. This wasn't some bizarre pre-race ritual but an attempt to scrub clean the track surface so that Valentino wouldn't get too sideways when he dumped the clutch at the start. HRC protested and Valentino was sent to the back of the grid.

Rossi seemed remarkably un-rattled by the whole thing, even if overtaking was considered almost impossible at Losail because the track was so slippery off the narrow racing line. On the grid he had 20 riders ahead of him, and there were real concerns that there might be another turn-one pile-up. Yet Valentino was sublime in the first few seconds of the race – up the inside, off the grippy line and past 11 of the world's greatest riders in one corner. No one could quite believe what they'd just seen. It was as if they had witnessed a miracle performed in the desert, like Rossi conforms to his own laws of physics, his own coefficients of grip.

Two laps later he was fourth, with back-on-form Gibernau still in sight in first place. Now this should have been a moment for calm reflection, for a spot of mental arithmetic, because he had already salvaged a great result from the direst of situations. But this wasn't the day Valentino proved he is god-like. It was the day he proved that he is merely human, beset by earthly emotions like that deadly desire for revenge.

At any other racetrack he might not have crashed. Valentino invariably kisses the grass between the kerb and the tarmac as he completes his exit from a corner. This time was no different, except Losail was bordered not by grass but by Astroturf, laid down in a vain attempt to keep sand off the tarmac. The instant Rossi's rear tyre touched the green plastic it kicked sideways and he was flung into the dirt. It was the biggest mistake of his career, by a long way, and he knew it. Limping away from the scene of the accident, blood oozing from his tattered left glove, he was very, very angry.

And not only with himself. After the race Valentino lashed out at race-winner Gibernau, who he suspected of involvement in HRC's protest, accusing him of being the classroom sneak. From now on Valentino started to really hate his old friend, just like he had hated Biaggi, their eyes never meeting when they were side by side in press conferences or on the podium. 'I've been looking for an excuse not to talk to Sete,' he snarled. 'Sete is behind all this, he's behaved like a child.' Whatever, Valentino had made a major mess of things – with just three races to go his 39-point advantage had suddenly shrunk to 14.

How to recover from such a monumental cock-up? His title teetering on the brink, Valentino had to make sure that his anger didn't get on the wrong side of him again. He had plenty of time for contemplation during the flight home to Europe (to have his injured finger fixed) and then back out east for the following Sunday's Malaysian GP. During those long hauls he nurtured and honed that lust for revenge, arriving at Sepang looking more serious than he'd ever done. This time he wasn't racing just for fun. 'I wanted to destroy the morale of everybody,' he said after leaving his rivals floundering in the steamy tropical heat.

On his victory lap Valentino displayed both the light and dark sides of his character – stopping to scrub clean the track with a broom handed to him by a member of his fan club and then dissing Gibernau. The Spaniard had stopped to congratulate the race winner but Vale ignored him. It had been another miserable weekend for Gibernau who had only managed a seventh-place finish. Valentino couldn't resist adding insult to injury: 'For me, Sete did his best race of the season. He has given me a lot of points which is like a big present. I am really grateful.' Or as JB put it: 'When Sete drops his bottom lip, he really drops his bottom lip.'

On to Phillip Island for the penultimate race where a second-place finish would be enough to secure the title. Gibernau was digging deep again in Australia, taking pole just ahead of the blue M1. Even though he knew victory might not be enough to keep the title open for the final round at Valencia, Gibernau desperately wanted to beat Valentino in Australia. His morale depended on it. No wonder that he took off like a scalded cat to end the first lap over a second ahead, while Valentino pulled off one of the most remarkable saves of his career, followed seconds later by an amazing double pass – he ran onto the dirt out of the 120mph turn eight, saved it, then passed both Ducatis into the MG hairpin, two corners later. Another glimpse of genius. After that he stalked the leading RCV, then made his move on the final lap. He got ahead but then ran wide, allowing Gibernau back in front. Somehow he once again found room where no one else can, slipping past into the rapid Hayshed sweeper to win his 40th premier-class GP by 0.097 seconds. Rossi had won his fourth consecutive crown and become only the second man in history to win back-to-back titles in the big class (after Eddie Lawson, who made a winning switch from Yamaha to Honda in 1989).

And Yamaha had won its first title since 1992, prompting this eulogy from Gauloises Yamaha technical director Ichiro

Yoda. 'In my experience Rossi is the greatest,' said Yoda, a long-time Yamaha man who has worked with some of the best riders in history: King Kenny Roberts, Eddie Lawson and Wayne Rainey. 'Rossi can lead everyone – he leads the engineers, the mechanics, the crew chief, so his influence is very big. He finds the correct direction and we follow him, so we can make quick developments. This year with Rossi we find out that racing is very easy! He is so easy to work with. With him everything is black or white, grey never exists. We've never before worked with a rider like this, even King Kenny. Rossi is very different, he is always very calm, he is always a gentleman, he never shouts, he always smiles. Plus he also has a big passion for winning – with him winning is everything. I have no idea how he does it – he is a genius.'

And then to Spain for the final race. Now you might have expected Valentino to give himself a weekend off but not a bit of it. He worked as hard as ever to win his ninth race of the year at Valencia (equalling his 2003 tally with the RCV) after overcoming a major straight-line speed disadvantage. This time he wasn't just sixth or seventh quickest through the speed trap, he was 14th. In other words more than half the grid had faster bikes, but not one of them could stop him in the race.

Just three days later he was back in action at Valencia, evaluating an all-new M1. JB was immediately impressed. 'It's already looking pretty ominous for the opposition,' he said. Valentino's input hadn't only helped Yamaha win the title, it was also helping the factory to build better racing bikes. Meanwhile HRC was floundering, losing its development direction as it fired new parts at all and sundry.

But the big question was still there: how long would Valentino stick around in bikes? Ferrari was making increasingly keen overtures, company president Luca di Montezemolo insisting that he was prepared to give Rossi a drive whenever he was ready to make the switch to four wheels. 'We will always think about a future with Valentino,' said di Montezemolo. 'There will always be an open door for him at Ferrari. He is a great champion, he is also young and therefore has a lot of time if he wants to move to F1.'

If he does go to F1 in 2007, Rossi will start his four-wheel career at the age of 28. Conventional wisdom suggests that would be far too late to change sports successfully. But after his 2004 season you have to wonder – is there anything that this man would find impossible?

Chapter 10

HOW ROSSI RIDES

G rand prix bikes are the baddest-assed motorcycles on Earth because they've got more brakes, more grip, more rigid chassis and, most crucially, more horsepower than anything else. Valentino has to constantly juggle body weight and throttle input to get his Yamaha M1 on to the fattest part of the tyre, so he can rip as much horsepower as possible through that contact patch, all the while keeping the rear tyre spinning, not too little, not just too much. Too little wheelspin means he's not laying down enough power and not helping the bike to turn, too much wheelspin and he's losing forward drive or he's about to have a highside.

Like only the greatest racers, Valentino keeps the thing dancing on that precipice, using everything just as hard as he can, so if he braked any later, cornered any faster, accelerated any harder, he'd go over the edge. Like any pro-racer, he makes a living out of being given an inch and trying to make it a mile, but his own personal precipice is many miles on from our own, and even out there his control is so much more deft, even when the bike's skipping and sliding beneath him, like it does into every corner, through every corner and out of every corner.

Someone like Valentino inhabits a world that's difficult to compare with our own because his experience of bike riding is so alien to ours, but maybe you can have a go at imagining for a moment that you're a GP rider. Let's say that you're in the closing stages of the British GP and you're rocketing into the first turn at 155mph, there's someone to the left of you and someone to the right, the guy on the right has just barged past and nicked your line, brakes squealing, suspension juddering, tyres chattering as he ricochets off your bike and nearly rips your right hand off the 'bars.

Your front tyre is tucking, pushing and sliding as you tip into the turn, so you're thrusting your right knee deep into the tarmac to keep some weight off the over-worn tyre, at the same time as you're thinking about getting on the throttle. You crack the throttle a fraction, just to get the revs building and take some more weight off the front, then you open it some more, until you can feel the rear tyre loading up, then you open it some more until you feel the revs rise and the tyre getting all greasy and braking loose, so you ease off and push like a bastard on the outside footpeg until the rubber regains some traction, which you immediately eat up by getting back on the throttle, which pushes the bike wide until you're on the rumble strip, so you ease off again as the tyre jumps, spins and kicks back across the kerb. Now you're pushing back in the seat to get more weight on that rear tyre and weighting the 'pegs to complete the cornering arc to the right, which takes you back on to the tarmac where the rear tyre grips and kicks the front wheel into the air, so you pull your weight over the front of the bike, easing the throttle for a millisecond, trying to get the front back on the tarmac as you head down towards Craner Curves, your hands, feet, backside and brain in some kind of a St Vitus dance of a balancing act as you lean hard right at 130mph, all of three feet behind the guy who's just overtaken you.

That's one breathless snapshot of maybe five seconds in a GP that lasts 45 minutes. In other words, a GP is just like that, except repeated about 550 times, and I've mentioned only the most basic inputs that a rider uses through each and every corner. The really scary thing is that a rider like Valentino has made the most intricate of adjustments to all of those inputs every time he's switched bikes, from 125s to

250s, from 250s to 500s and from 500s to 1,000cc four-strokes. Somehow he has been able to reach into his subconscious, then override and reconfigure each facet of his riding technique, and all this while all hell is breaking loose on the racetrack.

His achievement is unique in bike racing history. In more than 50 years of GPs only one other rider has secured the triple crown of 125, 250 and 500 titles and that was Briton Phil Read, who took ten years to conquer the different classes, almost twice as long as the youngster. Valentino's ability to adapt so quickly marks him out as a superman among supermen, and one of the most versatile riders ever. So what is this talent with which he is blessed?

Every rider has his own style, his own way of controlling a motorcycle via throttle control, body weight and maximising traction. But different types of motorcycle require very different techniques to extract maximum performance from their engines and chassis. Valentino has the ability to swap seamlessly from one bike to another because he's been riding all kinds of bikes for 20 years, because he inherited the right genes from his GP-winning dad and because he's a bit of a genius. He's not quite unique, of course, men like King Kenny Roberts ruled American dirt track before conquering 500 GPs, and Sixties' legend Mike Hailwood could win three different GP classes in a day, though the specifics of different racing categories were less back then. But most riders are much less able to achieve the same level of competitiveness with different types of machine – witness the many 250 and Superbike stars who have failed to reinvent themselves as 500 or MotoGP heroes. These riders develop their skills and technique as they master a particular type of machine, but when they change classes, their style won't change with them.

Riding technique is a largely subconscious function, so it's hard to know exactly what you're doing a lot of the time, because there's so much going on when you're teetering on the limit, duelling with a rival. To be able to adapt the way you brake, turn, accelerate, shift your body weight and so on therefore demands a very special mind. Valentino, being a modest guy, shrugs it all off. 'Racing 125s was like a game, 250s were serious, but 500s are very serious!' he said halfway through his first 500 season. 'They're dangerous: you open the throttle and you've got almost 200 horsepower, so you have to be careful …'

Niall Mackenzie, who won the British 250 title, then went on to score several 500 GP podiums before returning to dominate the national Superbike scene, believes Valentino's secret is threefold: his lack of an 'I know best' ego which allows him to look, listen and learn, his ability to rear-wheel steer and his refusal to hang around in any one class too long.

'The longer you stay on one kind of bike, the harder it is to change,' says Mackenzie. 'Rossi wasn't on 250s too long and even when he was he looked like he was already thinking about how to ride 500s. He seems prepared to change how he rides, while most other riders decide their way is the only way.

'When I was riding 500s I'd be competitive if the bike or my style suited the track but that doesn't work every week, you have to be able to adapt and that's where the Americans and Australians scored when I was riding, and where Rossi scores now. They ride the rear wheel because you can give the rear so much more abuse and get away with it. If you rely on the front there's such a fine line between the tyres gripping, to allow you to keep up your corner speed, and crashing. On a 125 you can push the front all day long, maybe a little less on a 250, but 500s and MotoGP bikes push the front so much harder, because you've got more weight and a huge rear-tyre contact patch.'

Californian Wayne Rainey, who won three 500 titles while Mackenzie struggled to get the best out of 500s, was the master of slide. 'As a kid, being sideways was as normal as riding in a straight line,' says Rainey, who grew up doing US dirt track. 'When I started roadracing in the early Eighties, I didn't know if sliding was right or wrong but it was what I felt comfortable with. If the tyre wasn't spinning and the bike turning, I didn't feel right. I liked it spinning because it gives you a safety buffer, you kinda know where you can go with it.

'In fact, sliding is the easy part, the difficult part is front-tyre feel. The key to my riding style was getting through that area really quick, getting the front tyre out of the way so I could get on the throttle. When you brake and flick, it's all front tyre, which is kinda risky. The advantage rear-wheel steering gave me was huge. And it's just the same now – watch Rossi, he's getting a bit sideways now. It's great when you've a lot of grip because you can use more throttle than the other guys, and then when the grip starts to fade, you know where the traction is.

'To me the throttle was everything. But when you're doing this you're talking very small changes in throttle opening because you're at the limit of everything – throttle position, chassis flex, tyre flex, you're feeling all that stuff. Spinning the rear relieves pressure on the tyre, relieves pressure on the suspension and that widens the safety area. But you're only spinning to keep the bike turning, just to keep it on track. Most of the time you don't want the tyre to spin much at all, you want it to drive maximum, you're always focused on drive.'

Valentino's mentor, Mick Doohan, played his part in helping the youngster adapt to big bikes but the former 500 champ insists that Valentino did most of the work himself. 'He has studied everyone, from Freddie Spencer to the guys he races against now,' says Doohan. 'He looks at them all on TV and works out the best way to ride. He's watched so many races on video that he probably knows them better than the statistics guys. He watches, he thinks and he listens to others.

I told him a few things early on – not to keep the bike on its side so much, just get it into the turn, get it up and get it out – but it didn't take him long to catch on.'

Whatever his god-given talent, Valentino needed to change his riding style when he came to 500s. He'd grown up through 125s and 250s, where corner speed is king, and while corner speed is also crucial in big-bike racing, it's not the way to ride from start to finish. A 200-plus horsepower motorcycle burns up its tyres during a race, so the sidegrip that is there in the early laps isn't there later on. Watch Valentino accelerate out of a turn and he does exactly what Doohan advised him to do – he lifts the bike, almost violently, as he brings on the throttle, which gives him a larger tyre-to-tarmac contact patch that can handle bigger throttle openings.

Adjusting to that corner-exit style requires the rider to use less corner speed, so he's got to adapt by slowing down, obviously a very difficult thing for any racer to do since this is the opposite of their remit. To succeed on a 500 or MotoGP bike you must breach that mental barrier and slow your corner entry so you can focus on corner exit, raise the bike on to the fatter section of its rear tyre and then open that throttle, little by little. That's how Valentino transformed himself from 250 winner to big-bike king, by using less corner speed, much more intricate throttle control and a willingness to adapt his technique throughout the race, according to fuel load and tyre wear.

'It's really difficult because your head's telling you that the rear-end style seems slow,' continues Mackenzie. 'In a race you're in an intense, urgent situation, so you're just thinking "Fast, fast, keep going fast!", your brain is telling you to rush into corners, so you're pushing the front for more corner speed. You've got to force yourself to slow down but you're thinking "Using the rear and not pushing the front is slow, if I do that I'm going to lose time and places".

'Somehow you've got to have some kind of mechanism within yourself to override what feels fast and what is fast, that's the clever bit, that's the tricky bit. Guys like Rainey and Doohan could ride the rear too, because it came naturally from riding the dirt. If you can force yourself to keep riding the rear, eventually you'll go faster, although the longer you've been doing high corner speed, the harder it is to stop.'

Which brings us to Max Biaggi. Rossi's arch-rival challenged for the 2001 500 title after three wins at tracks well suited to his high corner speed style but his brave effort collapsed after three copycat front-end crashes. The theory goes that Biaggi stayed in 250s too long, lording it over his rivals with the number-one plate, so that by the time he got to 500s he couldn't change (although he'd argue that he challenged Doohan for the title in his first 500 season, when he was riding Hondas, suggesting it's his Yamaha that was at fault).

'Biaggi is a very hard 250 rider and he's also very good on 500s and MotoGP bikes,' says Valentino. 'But you never see him slide the rear because he uses the front so much. When I started 500s I also used the front very much and I crashed many times.'

Mackenzie likens Rossi's adaptability to that of Doohan, who won five 500 titles after a near-crippling accident which left him more disabled than he ever lets on. 'Rossi's ability to think and adapt compares to the way Mick coped with his right foot not moving. He forced himself to adapt, to ride the bike with a really weak right leg and with no movement in his right ankle. Most other riders would say: "I just can't do this, it's not physically possible". It's hard enough to ride a big bike when you're 100 per cent, so it's easy to say "I can't ride it properly now", but Doohan forced his way around that.'

Valentino admits to using Doohan's riding style as a reference point, but he didn't simply copy every aspect of the grand master's technique. 'Mick used to slide and go, like a real 500 rider, and his settings didn't have to be so exact because of that,' he explains. 'But I came from 250s so I had to change my style to go into corners a little slower, and though I learned to understand slide control and started to slide like Mick, I'm still faster in the middle of the corner, not because I'm a better rider, just because I have a different technique.'

Nevertheless, Doohan has nothing but praise for Rossi's technique: 'I think Valentino is the only guy who rides right at the moment. The rest of them ride like they're on 250s, so when the tyres go off they've got no answer, their only answer is to roll off the throttle. In qualifying, everyone goes quick because they've got fresh tyres and low fuel loads, but come halfway through the race, when the front tyre starts to push and the rear starts to spin, they've got to slow down but Valentino adjusts his riding style to accommodate the change in grip, moving his body weight differently and using the throttle differently. That's where he's got it, that's why he's consistently quick from lap one to lap 30.'

Mackenzie is amazed that Valentino mastered sideways corner exits so quickly. 'He seems to slide the rear so easily, though he's got a very ordinary riding style, like some guy at a track day, but he's obviously using his weight, balance and throttle control. It's pretty obvious what he was doing on the 500 during 2001. He'd be with them for the first half of the race, watching, waiting and probably pretty much at his limit. But during the second half, when everyone else's fronts were shot, so they couldn't push hard anymore, then he'd start riding the rear.'

Valentino's rear-wheel-steering ability is the result of a very special natural talent that has been honed since the day he first rode a minibike aged two and a half. Again, he shrugs it off: 'I think my throttle control is just natural. I started very young and rode many bikes but I don't know why I have this style of control. When me and Loris Capirossi were racing 250s for Aprilia, he used the throttle like a switch, on or off, I use more gentle control, but he was usually just as fast.' Maybe on 250s, but Valentino's ultra-delicate throttle control makes all the difference when you're dealing with double the horsepower. When he came to 500 GPs in 2000 it took just a couple of races before his data-logging traces told Honda that his throttle control was far superior to that of their more experienced factory riders like Capirossi, Alex Criville and Tady Okada.

But Valentino's corner-exit secret isn't just throttle control. It's also the intricate feel he possesses, so he knows what the rear tyre is going to do, almost before it does it.

'To slide like they do, MotoGP riders need a huge amount of feel and feedback,' explains Michelin's bike racing boss Nicolas Goubert. 'They need to sense exactly what the tyre is doing, and from experience, know what it's going to do next. Tyre compound and, to a lesser extent, construction are the crucial factors in offering excellent feedback.

'The more grip a rider has at his disposal, the more feel and feedback he needs. What most riders want is a period of warning as they approach the limit. It's no good having massive amounts of grip if the limit is reached without any warning, because the rider won't have the confidence to approach that limit. Most riders will go faster with slightly less grip and more feedback. Only the very best riders can go fastest with a huge amount of grip and minimal feedback, because their special skill allows them to cope with less of a transition phase.'

Superbike star Chris Walker's fated attempt to conquer the 500 class in 2001 was spent in awe of men like Valentino. 'When I followed good 500 guys into corners, I could sometimes run up on them a little, even the best riders out there. But by the time I came out of the turn, they were halfway down the next straight! The good 500 guys seem to turn the corner more, then pick up the bike and get on the gas really hard. With Superbikes you spend a lot more time on your side, so on the 500 I'd find I was always leant over further than anyone else. With a four-stroke you can actually get on the power while the bike is on its side. A Superbike weighs more, so there's more weight on the tyres when it's leaned over, so there's obviously more grip, and the power is less aggressive, much smoother, so you can drive out of the corner. The 500 is very different – they're so aggressive when the power comes on tap, that you go from good grip to zero grip virtually instantly.'

That's the real difference between a hard man and a hero, between a good MotoGP rider and a legend: super-intricate throttle control that allows the rider to unleash maximum horsepower impossibly early out of every corner. Valentino has dedicated most of his life to honing that skill and now reaps the rewards.

Chapter 11

ROSSI'S WEAPONS

From zero to hero

Yamaha YZR-M1 2004/2005

Yamaha's YZR-M1 was MotoGP's most maligned motorcycle until Valentino Rossi came along. During the first two seasons of four-stroke MotoGP racing the M1 won just two races, while Honda's RC211V won 28 victories (20 of those with Valentino on board) and both world titles. It didn't seem like there was anything right about the M1 – riders criticised its lack of speed and acceleration, its fickle handling, its loose front end and its instability, especially towards the end of races. No wonder former GP winner Randy Mamola, who did a back-to-back M1 versus RCV test after the 2003 season, told Valentino: 'Man, you're f**ked!'

MotoGP bikes are the world's fastest racing motorcycles – 240 horsepower, 210mph and bullet-like acceleration. Most of the factories struggled to build user-friendly machines during the first few years of the four-stroke formula that had its inaugural season in 2002. Honda was the only company that got it right from the outset – its RCV was both hugely fast and very manageable. Yamaha engineers eventually admitted they got the M1 wrong because they hadn't realised just how fast the 990cc four-strokes would be, they'd only designed their bike to beat the old-school 500cc two-strokes, which still shared the tracks with the four-strokes in 2002.

If the M1's first season was pretty miserable – just two wins from 16 races – 2003 was a disaster. The bike didn't win a single race and scored just one podium finish. Many people thought Valentino had taken leave of his senses when he quit Honda and signed to ride the M1 in October 2003.

The challenge was enormous but Yamaha was already getting its act together before it secured the World Champ's services. The company had appointed a new boss in the spring of 2003, Masao Furosawa, who immediately instigated bold new plans to attack Honda's superiority. So while Valentino's riding skills are generally acknowledged as the most significant factor in the M1's transformation from loser to winner, the bike's three main performance factors – engine, electronics and chassis – all underwent significant changes for 2004.

'My target was to combine all the technology available in Yamaha, to become much more scientific and not so intuitive,' says Furosawa. 'When I first worked in MotoGP I realised that engine horsepower isn't the most important factor in achieving victory. The reality is good power delivery to the rear tyre, that's much more important than power itself.'

Although Yamaha stayed faithful to its favoured inline-four engine configuration (which allows a shorter wheelbase and better weight distribution compared to the vee configuration engines used by Honda, Ducati and Suzuki) the 2004 M1 engine was internally very different. Biggest change was the switch from Yamaha's trademark five-valve cylinder heads and even firing intervals to four-valve heads and uneven firing intervals. 'We started work on this engine during the spring of 2003,' reveals M1 project leader Masahiko Nakajima. 'For winter testing we built four engines with four different combinations of valve configuration and firing interval. Valentino immediately preferred the four-valve, uneven firing engine. We always knew that four valves give a milder taste, while five valves give a sharper taste.' The uneven firing intervals also help create a tamer machine by applying power pulses to the rear tyre in a more effective way. No one is exactly sure why, but the most popular theory suggests that uneven power pulses give the rear tyre a chance to maintain traction during vicious acceleration. Rossi described the new engine as 'more sweet' than the 2003 M1.

Mildness and sweetness are obviously relative terms, but when you're dealing with 240 horsepower you want those 240 horses to be as friendly as possible. Which is why Yamaha switched to that new configuration engine, even though it was initially slower than the 2003 motor. By May's French GP Yamaha had equipped Rossi with a more powerful four-valve, uneven firing order motor, which was fast enough to propel him to 212mph at June's Italian GP where he won the first of a hat-trick of victories that put him on course for World Championship glory.

In addition to internal engine improvements Yamaha also worked hard to help Rossi put all the power to the ground by developing the M1's electronic systems – EMS (engine management system) which includes TCS (traction control system) and ICS (idle control system). The factory forged new links with F1 electronics experts Magneti Marelli who supplied hardware and operations systems, while Yamaha created its own software applications.

The 2004 TCS wizardry was much more intelligent than the M1's 2003 system. It controlled wheelspin via engine and chassis sensors which monitor factors like lean angle and slip angle (via gyros and triple-axis sensors) to control wheelspin according to tyre wear and track conditions. 'We worked hard to get a very natural control from this system because it's not good if the rider can feel the electronic control,' adds Nakajima. 'TCS helps the rider improve his speed out of the corners.'

The 2004 ICS (which controls idle speed to assist the M1's slipper clutch in maintaining rear-end stability during braking) was also cleverer than its predecessor, taking real-time inputs that adapt during the race to changing track conditions and increasing tyre wear.

Chassis development followed a similar theme – to improve rider feeling, allowing riders to attack the corners with more confidence and thus greater speed. The 2004 M1 chassis was softened to reduce lateral rigidity for better feedback into turns and lazier slides out of turns. Then engine hangers were added either side of the engine to maintain the chassis' vertical and twist rigidity, for good braking control and sharp steering. Meanwhile crew chief Jeremy Burgess worked on adjusting chassis geometry after realising that the M1 needed raising and lengthening. 'During our early tests we weren't getting enough weight transfer to the front or to the rear,' says JB. 'We identified fairly early on that our braking distances were too long because we weren't getting the weight onto the "top" of the tyre, we were more or less pushing from behind, so we lifted the bike. This also helped turning in longer corners because it gets the weight further inside. Of course, if you go higher you need to go longer for the overall balance. If you don't, it'll steer like a boat and, conversely, if you go high and stay short the bike will be very unstable.'

That set-up, which increased front-end stability and corner-exit drive – was good enough for Rossi to win first time out in South Africa but more was required once the Honda hordes were up to speed. 'After Valentino won at Catalunya, Mugello and Assen, where we thought we'd suffer on the straights, we started to think anything was possible,' Burgess continues. 'But then we got rudely awakened at Rio.'

The M1 was an animal on Rio's bumps and then again next time out in Germany. M1 technical chief Ichiro Yoda: 'We think the snappiness comes from the bike's agility. Our bike has more agility than the others, which works for us at some tracks, against us at others. After Germany we worked on spring balance and damping to further improve overall balance and weight transfer.' From then on the M1's base set-up didn't change drastically, though the rear suspension still wasn't quite right.

The result of these multiple changes to engine, chassis and electronics was a supremely agile and useable motorcycle from which Rossi was able to extract maximum performance. 'Like Jeremy sometimes says, the bike is a tool, so we have to work to get the best out of the tool,' says Valentino. 'So when I have a problem, then we come up with an answer. If we have a problem with the front end, we modify the front end. It's like mathematics!

'We always knew it was possible to make a good result in my first year with Yamaha. From working with JB and the rest of my crew at Honda I knew I could be fast everywhere if I didn't make any mistakes. But my original idea for the 2004 season was a top-three finish – to win the title in the first year was fantastic.'

Yamaha YZR-M1 2004
Engine specifications

Type	liquid-cooled 16-valve parallel four-cylinder four-stroke
Displacement	990cc
Fuel system	fuel injection
Claimed output	over 240 horsepower
Gearbox	six-speed, cassette type

Chassis specifications

Frame type	dual beam aluminium
Tyres	Michelin
Wheels	16.5in front, 16.5in rear
Front brake	4-pot Brembo, twin carbon discs (dry), twin cast iron discs (wet)

Rear brake	2-pot Brembo, single disc
Front suspension	upside down Showa, multi-adjustable
Rear suspension	Ohlins with rising rate linkage, multi-adjustable
Race weight	over 145kg

Rossi's new world

Honda RC211V 2002/2003

Honda made its name winning GPs with exotic four-stroke race bikes in the sixties, so the success of its RC211V four-stroke MotoGP bike came as no great surprise. The world's biggest bike manufacturer has always been a four-stroke brand. Indeed company founder Soichiro Honda hated smelly, smoky two-strokes so much that his engineers used to explain away two-stroke blueprints that he might find in his R&D department as lawnmower engines.

Honda's speciality was exotica. During the sixties the company's engineers produced a twin-cylinder 50cc GP bike, a five-cylinder 125 and a 250 six, all revving beyond 20,000rpm; no wonder Honda's first nine years of GP racing yielded 16 riders' World Championships, 18 constructors' crowns and 138 victories. But during the seventies two-stroke technology advanced to the extent that not even Honda could compete with its outrageous 32 valve, oval-pistoned NR500 four-stroke, so the company went with the two-stroke flow, winning a further 25 riders' titles and 35 constructors' crowns between 1983 and 2001.

In 2002 Honda was back to doing what it does best thanks to a transformation of Grand Prix regulations designed to put four-strokes out front and consign two-strokes to the history books. This seismic shift was somewhat inevitable, given the environmental concerns that have marginalised the two-stroke engine as a practicable power source for streetbikes. The four-stroke MotoGP series thus brought the world's premier race series in line with the global street market, delivering more direct feedback to streetbike development and allowing factories to more fully exploit their racing success in the marketplace.

The MotoGP rules admitted 990cc four-strokes to GP racing, giving them engines twice as big as the 500cc two-strokes that had dominated the 500 class since the mid-seventies. But Valentino wasn't an immediate convert to the four-stroke cause. During his two seasons with his NSR500 two-stroke he developed a deep love for the bike's razor-edged power delivery and initially found the easier-going RCV uninspiring to ride. Then he checked the lap times …

Short, stubby and very businesslike, the 2002 RCV was the most powerful Grand Prix bike ever built. The five-cylinder vee made a booming off-kilter racket and produced around 220 horsepower, maybe 30 more than the NSR that Rossi raced to the 2001 500 championship, so it didn't take long for him to surpass his NSR lap times.

'The RCV is incredible,' he said in the spring of 2002. 'The first time I tested it at Suzuka after the Eight Hour in July 2001 it was a bit of a disaster, the bike was too small, many things weren't right for me. The second time, at Jerez in November, it wasn't very good. But we made a good test; I'm good at understanding what I want from the bike and HRC are very good at giving me what I want. After the Jerez tests everything basically changed: the engine character, all the electronic parts, the cowling, the seat, it's a new bike and it's very fast.'

Rossi's only gripe was the bike's rather meagre Manga cartoon-inspired bodywork. He kept complaining about its meagre fairing, and so would you at 200mph. Despite improvements the RCV does look seriously unaerodynamic even now, but is it? In some ways, yes, in some ways, no. The kind of swoopy bodywork required to slice through the air in a straight line actually compromises performance in other areas, causing instability during braking and cornering, especially in high-speed turns. The tight, angular fairing therefore improves lap times even if it may lose a few tenths at the very end of a main straight.

The RCV is a distillation of everything that Honda has learned from racing in almost half a century of competition, and yet the bike's V5 configuration was anything but an obvious choice for the new four-stroke championship. But Honda has always believed that taking the more difficult road can earn them greater knowledge, though this insistence on being different has sometimes cost them dear. Back in the late seventies they tried to take on the all-dominant two-stroke 500s with the NR and never scored a single World Championship point despite blowing billions of yen. Then in the mid-eighties their first NSR500 ran its fuel tank under the engine, with the aim of lowering the centre of gravity, but the bike was a disaster.

'We aim to prove that Honda technology is better than the easy way, like an inline four,' says Honda Racing Corporation director Yasuo Ikenoya. 'People ask us why we choose the difficult way but the answer is simple: racing is meant to be a challenge, and racing is in Honda's DNA. Of course, we considered other configurations. A V4 would be good – short and narrow – but a V4 is not interesting to us!'

Jeremy Burgess reckons Honda were ahead from the start of MotoGP because they didn't compromise when they designed the RCV. 'I really think that it's better to start with a clean sheet of paper, then you don't have to make any compromises,' he says. 'Honda started from nowhere when they began work, then they did enough research to see what's the best tool to work within the regulations. Yamaha and Suzuki both shoehorned their four-stroke motors into modified 500 chassis, and that's a compromise.'

The straight-talking Aussie, who was never afraid to tell his Japanese bosses what he thought when they do get things wrong, also believed that HRC were correct in choosing a five-cylinder engine. MotoGP regs have a sliding scale of minimum weight limits: the more cylinders, the higher the minimum weight, but fours and fives share the same 145 kilo limit. 'If you can run the same weight as a four, you might as well have a five. So the five was definitely the right way to go.'

Honda also considered building a V6 but the four-stroke regs place a further ten kilo weight handicap on bikes using six or more cylinders. Honda has heavily emphasised the concept of total balance with the RCV. 'Total balance' is racing's current buzz phrase and isn't difficult to grasp. Outright horsepower isn't the way to win races nowadays, especially in four-stroke GPs, because all the bikes have more than enough horsepower. What counts is how that power is made to work with the rest of the bike – the chassis and, most crucially, the tyres.

'The RCV combines all our racing experience to combine optimum power with good machine control,' Ikenoya goes on. 'There are three elements to our total balance concept: concentration of mass, minimal frontal area and optimum traction. All the riders that have ridden the bike have been impressed by its power and compactness.'

Compactness is a driving force with the RCV, hence the narrowish vee angle of 75.5 degrees. The more compact you make the motor, the more room you have to put the engine where you want it, focusing the centre of mass.

HRC have further followed that concept by mounting the fuel tank as low as possible. That's obviously what Honda were trying to do when they built the 'upside-down' NSR500 in '84, but they went too far that time. Instead of gaining from a low c of g, they suffered for it, because their engineers didn't realise that pitch is crucial for adjusting traction between the front and rear tyres as the rider goes in and out of a corner.

The RCV's fuel tank isn't that low; it's positioned very centrally, partly under the front of the seat, a clever feature that helps to banish the excessive pitch suffered by machines with conventional tanks, especially on full fuel loads early in the race.

'In the past all our riders have complained about riding with full fuel tanks,' adds Ikenoya. 'You could see that Rossi was always very fast at the end of races when his NSR500's fuel load was less – we wanted him to be fast from the early laps and the RCV's fuel tank design helps in this way.'

It would be a gross understatement to suggest that the RCV is easy to ride, but the bike is certainly less demanding than the old NSR, which is why the new breed of four-strokes are generally quicker around a racetrack than 500s.

'The four-stroke is easier because when you're mid-corner on a 500 you have zero power,' explains Burgess. 'When you open the throttle from the lowest rpm point, say 6000, the 500's not making any more power than a streetbike but then it suddenly builds to 190 horsepower. With the four-stroke you touch the throttle mid-corner and you've still got tons of torque, so from that point you can open the throttle fairly quickly, whereas with two-stroke you have to be really careful how you open the throttle. Plus the engine is just bloody fast, there's so much power that you can just drive past a 500, even on a short straight.'

In fact the four-stroke's advantages go even deeper than that. Four-strokes have much more engine braking than two-strokes, which gives better traction and improved feel on a closed throttle. We'll leave a rival engineer, Garry McCoy's former crew chief Hamish Jamieson to explain this one. 'I think there's a few reasons why four-strokes are easier,' says Jamieson. 'They're heavier for a start, which makes them easier, because they're less flighty. They've more weight and inertia, so they're less of a handful to control, while 500s are barely touching the ground half the time, so they've got no grip.

'In the Red Bull Yamaha team we had a good example in Nori Haga coming to 500s from Superbikes in 2001. He found the 500 difficult to turn in because there's no engine braking. A 500 doesn't slow down with stability from the rear the way a four-stroke does. Getting a 500 stopped and turned is difficult because the bike just wants to go straight on, and if you get the front to stop, the rear wants to come around. With a 500, there's this transition period when the rider has finished braking but he's not opened the throttle, so the bike's loose, it's not taut like a four-stroke, it's just running free, a bit out of control. That's why guys like Haga and Chris Walker struggled on 500s.'

But four-strokes aren't all good. According to minimum weight regulations the V5 must weigh 15 kilos more than a 500, and that's a huge difference in racetrack terms. 'And the weight is also in different places compared to the 500,' adds Burgess. 'So the RCV doesn't turn as fast as the 500 and Valentino can't flick it left and right so quick, plus it's fuel injected, so it's a whole new game.'

Of course, too much engine braking can be a bad thing, which is why HRC developed the so-called back-torque limiter for the high-revving NR500, to minimise rear-wheel hop into corners. The RCV uses a similar system, which caused a few problems in 2002 but has been gradually improved with electronics. Of course, RCV's five-cylinder configuration helps on engine braking. Some of Honda's four-stroke GP rivals have struggled with excessive engine braking unsettling their machines as they hurtle into corners, seriously affecting lap times. 'The five is definitely a help on engine braking,' adds Burgess. 'Way back I had an old Honda CB750 four road bike and I could kick start it with my hand, you couldn't do that with a Norton twin. It follows that you're going to have less compression at any one time if you've got five strokes per two engine revolutions rather than four, and that's got to help any engine-braking problems.'

If the RCV gave Rossi an easier ride on the racetrack, it also gave Burgess and his crew an easier time in the pits. No longer do mechanics have to fully strip and rebuild engines, as they did with the NSR, because RCV engines are prepared away from the racetrack. Also, the bike's fuel injection system means no more fiddling around with carburettor jets, and the four-stroke's wider rpm range means less mucking about with gearbox ratios. Easy life!

Honda RC211V 2003

Engine specifications

Type	liquid-cooled 20-valve 75.5 degree V5 four-stroke
Displacement	990cc
Fuel system	PGM fuel injection
Claimed output	220 to 240 horsepower
Gearbox	six-speed, cassette type

Chassis specifications

Frame type	dual beam aluminium
Tyres	Michelin
Wheels	17in front, 16.5in rear
Front brake	4-pot Brembo, twin carbon discs (dry), twin cast iron discs (wet)
Rear brake	2-pot Brembo, single disc
Front suspension	upside down Showa, multi-adjustable
Rear suspension	Pro-link with Showa shock, multi-adjustable
Wheelbase	1,440mm
Length	2,050mm
Race weight	over 145kg

Maximum respect

Honda NSR500 2000/2001

Valentino Rossi's Nastro Azzurro Honda NSR500 was the last and greatest of the two-stroke 500s that ruled Grand Prix racing for quarter of a century from 1975 to 2001. The machine was the apogee of the high-performance two-stroke racer, a 190 horsepower, 130 kilo surface-to-surface missile that could be safely and successfully guided only by the sharpest, bravest riders.

Rossi has more respect for the NSR than any other motorcycle he's ridden. 'I think it's necessary to have big balls to ride the 500,' he says. 'The four-strokes may be faster but for sure they don't give the same sensation. Yes, the satisfaction of riding the 500 was a very, very big motivation for me, because when you're riding the most difficult bike in the world, it's necessary to have a perfect set-up if you're to be able to ride fast, and you've also got to ride perfect all the time.'

By the time Rossi graduated to 500s in 2000, the NSR500 had been developed into the most successful 500 GP bike ever. Mick Doohan alone won 54 GPs on the bike between 1990 and '98, and Rossi's 14 500 wins took the NSR to 132 GP victories.

During his ten GP seasons, Mighty Mick helped make the NSR almost unbeatable but Rossi made the best bike in the world even better in his two years with the machine. The guy has divine riding talent and engineer Jeremy Burgess reckons his bike development skills exceed Micky D's. Remarkable for someone aged just 22.

'With Mick there was never much for us to do, because he'd win races by sheer mental and physical strength,' says Burgess. 'As long as the bike was about right, he could race it, he tended to put everything on himself. It's great with Valentino because he wants to work at making the bike better. I think it's because he came from 125s and 250s, where you have to get the most out of the machine to win. Mick came to 500s from Superbikes, which are less technically accurate.'

When Rossi quit Aprilia at the end of '99 to graduate to 500s with Honda, the NSR was losing its dominance. Alex Criville, who won the '99 500 title after Doohan smacked himself up, had taken Honda down the wrong road on engine development. The Spaniard had asked HRC for more horsepower (a mistake that many racers make) and that's the last thing the NSR needed. With more power the NSR got slower, not faster, because it became more difficult to ride. It was Rossi who saved the day.

'Valentino was like a new brain for Honda, his mind was unpolluted and uncluttered by some of the NSR phobias the other guys may have had,' adds Burgess. 'He gave clear and honest comments that gave the engineers something to get their teeth into. Because he was new to the bike, he wanted to work on things that Mick and Alex had got used to, because they'd always been that way. Also, Valentino rides different to Mick. He still has a bit of a 250 style, he doesn't hang off as far as Mick used to, and he ran the bike higher than Mick did, to get it steered.'

Honda pretty quickly realised that the young genius deserved a new NSR. 'The old bike had a lack of rear traction compared to the Yamaha and Suzuki, so Valentino would be spinning the rear rather than going forward,' Burgess continues. 'They built a new bike for the last few races of 2000, with the engine higher and further back for better acceleration traction.'

And traction, especially rear-end traction, is everything in big-bike racing, as former Suzuki engineer Warren Willing explains: 'To get the best race time out of a MotoGP bike you have to compromise, you mustn't abuse the tyres any more than necessary. It's about understanding the dynamics and the interaction that's going on between rider and bike and remembering that all the forces on the motorcycle are driven through the tyres. All the horsepower in the world doesn't equate to any force if it's not hooked up. It's all in the tyres: how the suspension affects them, how the engine affects them, the rider, the track temperature and so on.'

HRC's decision to shift the NSR's centre of mass didn't only improve the bike out of turns. 'The higher engine position also threw more weight on to the front during braking, improving traction into turns,' Burgess explains. 'Then we just played around with suspension and linkages to fix the speed of weight transfer from rear to front.'

Finally, the shift in overall balance also helped fix the NSR's oldest problem – understeer. The bike had always been known for drifting wide through corners, and that's one reason for Doohan's famous hunched-over-the-front riding style; he was desperately trying to get more weight up front.

Rossi, Burgess and HRC also worked at improving the NSR's already very linear power delivery. Like Doohan before him, Rossi prioritised a user-friendly mid-range over peak horsepower because 500 riding is all about meting out the power, and you can't do that if the power curve isn't right. That's why Rossi's 2001 NSR was equipped with uber-trick magnesium Keihins, of which there were only two sets in existence. No other Honda rider was deemed worthy of them.

Of course, even with that kind of help, 500 racing was always like riding the razor's edge for Rossi, and that's why he so loved his NSR. The new breed of GP four-strokes may be quicker but they don't give that same skating-on-the-edge-of-disaster feeling that racers crave. When a rider gets it right on a 500, he's climbed Mount Everest.

Chris Walker, who had a torrid crash-happy time with an NSR during 2001, puts it like this: 'If you go through a corner on a 500 and don't get it quite right and you think about it, you've missed the next turn! There's so much thinking, the trouble is that everything happens so fast. If you make a mistake, you're generally wearing it, whereas on a Superbike they give you some warning. On a 500, you miss a gear going into a corner and that's it, you've crashed. Do that on a Superbike and you'll probably be all right, you bang down the gears and find one, run wide and maybe touch the grass, but you get away with it. If you watch a 500 GP there's not many mistakes made because a mistake generally means a crash.'

Honda NSR500 2001

Engine specifications

Type	liquid-cooled V4 two-stroke, reed-valve induction, with adjustable ignition, exhaust control etc
Bore & stroke	54 x 54.5mm
Displacement	499cc
Fuel system	four 36mm magnesium Keihin carbs
Claimed output	195hp at 12,500rpm
Gearbox	six-speed, cassette type

Chassis specifications

Frame type	dual beam aluminium
Tyres	Michelin
Wheels	17in front, 16.5in rear
Front brake	four-pot Brembo, twin 320mm carbon discs (dry), twin cast-iron discs (wet)
Rear brake	two-pot Brembo, single 196mm disc
Front suspension	47mm upside down Showa, multi-adjustable
Rear suspension	Pro-Link with Showa shock, multi-adjustable
Wheelbase	1,400mm
Length	2,010mm
Race weight	131kg

Fast but fickle

Aprilia RSW250 1998/1999

Aprilia has enjoyed so much success over the past decade that it's easy to forget just how short a time the little Italian factory has been with us. The first Aprilia grand prix bike was built in 1985, a kind of backyard special using a Rotax 250 motor, and yet by the time Rossi won the 1999 250 crown the factory had won ten world titles and over 100 GPs in the 250 and 125 categories.

Like Soichiro Honda almost half a century before him, Aprilia founder Ivan Beggio is well into his racing, and it was Aprilia's track successes that quickly established the brand as a serious player in the Italian, and then the world, markets. Neither is there any doubt that the company's relationship with the two highest-profile Italian racers of recent years – Rossi and before him Max Biaggi – helped burn the marque into the public consciousness.

In turn, both Rossi and Biaggi have been lucky to have had Aprilia around. It is Italy's motorcycle industry that has helped foster so many Italian stars, and without Aprilia their climb to the top of the sport would almost certainly have been much more difficult. Good machinery is vital in motorsport, without it even the best riders can fail to make the most of their talent, so it's not inconceivable that Rossi and Biaggi would never have made it without Aprilia around.

Rossi was also lucky that the Aprilia RSW250 was the most competitive 250 when he graduated to the class in 1998. In fact, '98 was the factory's best-ever year in GP racing, the RSW winning all but one of the season's 15 races. It hadn't always been so, for although Aprilia's 250s had always been fast, they'd also been fragile and fickle.

Aprilia won its first 250 GP in 1987, with Loris Reggiani on board, but it wasn't until '92 that the bike became consistently competitive against its Japanese rivals, Biaggi, Reggiani and Frankie Chili all scoring famous victories over main rivals Honda. It was another two years before race wins were turned into championship wins, Biaggi dominating the '94, '95 and '96 campaigns before defecting to Honda.

The Aprilia's winning speed has always been attributed to one major factor – its intake system. While all the Japanese 250s – Honda's NSR, Yamaha's YZR and Suzuki's RGV – use reed-valve induction, the RSW uses disc-valve induction. Disc valves offer the opportunity for higher peak power output but with a trade-off in lower-rpm usability while reeds do the opposite, delivering heaps of user-friendly mid-range but rather strangling the engine at peak revs.

In its earlier days the Aprilia probably suffered more than it gained from its uniqueness, for while the bike was a rocketship in a straight line, with a maniacally fast pick-up, it was slow out of the corners because riders struggled to cope with the vicious power delivery. But as electronics developed during the nineties, that awkwardness was tamed, thanks to much-improved ignition systems and exhaust powervalves. GP racing's switch to unleaded fuel in '98 also calmed things down.

Nevertheless the RSW's powerband was still crazily narrow – with the real business tucked between 12,000 and 13,000rpm – so Rossi didn't find the RSW the easiest of machines to master in '98. While he was immediately fast on the bike, it chucked him off at every opportunity in their first season together. He crashed out of no less than four races in '98.

'I'm still riding my 250 like it's a 125,' said Rossi midway through his debut 250 season. 'I am trying to learn something from my team-mates Harada and Capirossi but it doesn't work to change your own style too much, everyone has their own way of riding a motorcycle. I ride very different from Harada and Capirossi. If you watch Harada he's so smooth and makes it look easy, so you try to do the same, but it doesn't work. At Jerez, when I was racing with Capirossi for the win, I tried to follow his lines, but that made me slower. Four laps from the end I went back to my own style, and I caught him a little.

'Harada is very clean while Capirossi brakes very, very hard all the way into the corner, then he goes very slow mid-corner, then he gets on the gas, hard! That's more like a 500 riding style, and I suppose he learned that from '95 and '96 when he was riding 500s. I don't brake so deep, I don't stop mid-corner and I'm a little more gentle on the gas – I have very much fear of the highside!' Even in their second year together, Rossi found the RSW a real handful in the wet, finishing a very uncharacteristic seventh and eighth in the two wet races of '99.

In fact, the Aprilia's bad behaviour can't wholly be blamed on its finicky engine configuration. It took years for factory engineers to get the bike's chassis fully sorted. Initially the RSW's twin-beam aluminium frame – ostensibly the same as its rivals – was too stiff, giving riders a scary, edgy feel which failed to induce confidence through some corners and at some circuits. No wonder Rossi found the NSR500 so easy to get on with when he quit Aprilia at the end of '99.

Aprilia RSW250 1999

Engine specifications

Type	liquid-cooled, 90° V-twin two-stroke, disc-valve induction, with adjustable ignition, exhaust control
Bore & stroke	54 x 54.5mm
Displacement	249.6cc
Fuel system	two 42mm DellOrto carbs
Claimed output	over 96hp at 12,500rpm
Gearbox	six-speed, cassette type

Chassis specifications

Frame type	dual beam aluminium
Tyres	Dunlop
Wheels	17in front and rear
Front brake	four-pot Brembo, twin 255/273mm carbon discs (dry), twin cast-iron discs (wet)
Rear brake	two-pot Brembo, single 190mm disc
Front suspension	42mm upside down Ohlins, multi-adjustable
Rear suspension	carbon swingarm with Ohlins shock, multi-adjustable
Wheelbase	1,270mm
Length	1,970mm
Race weight	96kg

Rossi's learner special

Aprilia RS125R 1995/1996/1997

Even the fastest 125 GP bikes aren't imposing machines, until you see a bunch of them involved in a scary mid-race encounter, their riders taking the kind of risks that would get them into serious trouble on a MotoGP bike. If MotoGP racing is a hi-tech confrontation between outrageously over-powerful surface-attack missiles, then 125 GP racing is good ol' fashioned hand-to-hand combat.

In 125s, it's not the bikes that are impressive, it's what the riders can do with them that's impressive. A 125 forgives where a 250 or MotoGP bike won't, so 125 racing is a great way for a rider to smooth off his roughest edges, before moving on to more demanding, more dangerous machines. In 125s throttle control is not very important, with less than 50 horsepower available you can take big greedy handfuls and (probably) get away with it.

Unlike in big-bike racing, throttle control isn't what really matters in 125s. What really matters is maintaining momentum, and that means super-fast corner entry and mid-corner speeds. That's why 125 riders are always bouncing off each other as they fight for the fast line. The bikes have so little power that you must never scrub off more speed through a turn than absolutely necessary. In fact they have so little power that 125 riders believe it's worth bringing a little bit of foot power into the equation, frantically paddling away from the start of each race.

Rossi learned plenty from his Aprilia 125. He spent four years on different versions of the tiny single, initially with a Sandroni special in the '94 Italian championship, then in the '95 Euro and Italian series, then in GPs, winning his first World Championship success at Brno in August '96, then dominating the following season to wrap up his first world title.

The 125's engine internals are very similar to the 250's with almost identical porting arrangements, but with only half the 250's horsepower, so the 125 rolls over and dies if it slips out of its powerband. To keep the bike moving well, Rossi had to play hard and fast with the ultra-close ratio gearbox, trying to keep the tacho around bouncing around in the 12 to 13,000rpm zone. That was agony in the old days, because the vibration caused havoc with a certain part of the male anatomy, but Aprilia generously added a countershaft balancer before Rossi came along.

Size is important in 125s, the smaller the better, which explains why Rossi's RSR tipped the scales at a puny 71 kilos, less than half the weight of a MotoGP bike. Everything about the bike is puny, from the miniscule aluminium twin-beam chassis (again, a shrunken version of its big brother 250) to the skinny Dunlop slicks. The RSR is a learner GP bike, so it's got to be easy to throw around and easy to dominate. And there can be no doubt that the bike helped Rossi on the path to big-bike glory.

Aprilia RS125R 1997

Engine specifications

Type	liquid-cooled, single-cylinder two-stroke, disc-valve induction, with adjustable ignition, exhaust control
Bore & stroke	54 x 54.5mm
Displacement	124.8cc
Fuel system	39mm DellOrto carb
Claimed output	over 45hp at 12,700rpm
Gearbox	six-speed, cassette type

Chassis specifications

Frame type	dual beam aluminium
Tyres	Dunlop
Wheels	17in front and rear
Front brake	four-pot Brembo, single carbon disc (dry), single cast-iron disc (wet)
Rear brake	two-pot Brembo, single steel disc
Front suspension	35mm upside down Ohlins, multi-adjustable
Rear suspension	aluminium swingarm with Ohlins shock, multi-adjustable
Wheelbase	1,250mm
Length	1,970mm
Race weight	71kg

CAREER STATISTICS

Abbreviations:
DNF – did not finish;
FL – fastest lap;
mech – machine failure

1989   First go-kart race

1990   Regional go-kart champion; nine race wins

1991   5th – Italian junior Go-kart Championship
Wins first minimoto race

1992   1st – Regional Minimoto Championship

1993   3rd – 125 Italian Sport Production Championship – Bike:
Lusuardi Cagiva Mito

1994   1st – 125 Italian Sport Production Championship – Bike:
Cagiva Mito
6th – 125 Italian Championship – Bike: Sandroni RS125R

1995   1st – 125 Italian Championship – Bike: Aprilia RS125R
3rd – 125 European Championship – Bike: Aprilia RS125R

1996

125 World Championship

Bike: AGV Aprilia RS125R

Date	Event	Grid	Race
31.3	Malaysian GP, Shah Alam	13th	6th
7.4	Indonesian GP, Sentul	18th	11th
21.4	Japanese GP, Suzuka	10th	11th
12.5	Spanish GP, Jerez	7th	4th
26.5	Italian GP, Mugello	8th	4th
9.6	French GP, Paul Ricard	13th	DNF, crash/FL
29.6	Dutch GP, Assen	8th	DNF, crash
7.7	German GP, Nürburgring	4th	5th
21.7	British GP, Donington Park	9th	DNF, mech
4.8	Austrian GP, A1-Ring	3rd	3rd
18.8	Czech GP, Brno	pole	1st
1.9	City of Imola GP, Imola	2nd	5th/FL
15.9	Catalan GP, Catalunya	5th	DNF, crash
6.10	Rio GP, Jacarepagua	11th	DNF, crash
20.10	Australian GP, Eastern Creek	12th	14th

Overall championship position: 9th

1997

125 World Championship

Bike: Nastro Azzurro Aprilia RS125R

Date	Event	Grid	Race
13.4	Malaysian GP, Shah Alam	pole	1st/FL
20.4	Japanese GP, Suzuka	7th	DNF, crash
4.5	Spanish GP, Jerez	6th	1st/FL
18.5	Italian GP, Mugello	3rd	1st
1.6	Austrian GP, A1-Ring	2nd	2nd/FL
8.6	French GP, Paul Ricard	3rd	1st
28.6	Dutch GP, Assen	pole	1st

6.7	City of Imola	pole	1st/FL
20.7	German GP, Nürburgring	pole	1st
3.8	Rio GP, Jacarepagua	2nd	1st/FL
17.8	British GP, Donington Park	4th	1st/FL
31.8	Czech GP, Brno	3rd	3rd
14.9	Catalan GP, Catalunya	4th	1st
28.9	Indonesian GP	4th	1st/FL
5.10	Australian GP, Phillip Island	3rd	6th

Overall championship position: 1st

1998

250 World Championship

Bike: Nastro Azzurro Aprilia RSW250

Date	Event	Grid	Race
5.4	Japanese GP, Suzuka	7th	DNF, mech
19.4	Malaysian GP, Johor	2nd	DNF, crash/FL
3.5	Spanish GP, Jerez	3rd	2nd
17.5	Italian GP, Mugello	4th	2nd
31.5	French GP, Paul Ricard	3rd	2nd
14.6	Madrid GP, Jarama	4th	DNF, crash
27.6	Dutch GP, Assen	3rd	1st
5.7	British GP, Donington Park	2nd	DNF, crash
19.7	German GP, Sachsenring	4th	3rd
23.8	Czech GP, Brno	2nd	DNF, crash
6.9	City of Imola GP, Imola	5th	1st
20.9	Catalan GP, Catalunya	2nd	1st/FL
4.10	Australian GP, Phillip Island	2nd	1st
25.10	Argentine GP, Buenos Aires	3rd	1st/FL

Overall championship position: 2nd

1999

250 World Championship

Bike: Nastro Azzurro Aprilia RSW250

Date	Event	Grid	Race
18.4	Malaysian GP, Sepang	pole	5th
25.4	Japanese GP, Motegi	11th	7th
9.5	Spanish GP, Jerez	3rd	1st
23.5	French GP, Paul Ricard	pole	DNF, mech/FL
6.6	Italian GP, Mugello	6th	1st/FL
20.6	Catalan GP, Catalunya	2nd	1st/FL
26.6	Dutch GP, Assen	pole	2nd/FL
4.7	British GP, Donington Park	3rd	1st
18.7	German GP, Sachsenring	pole	1st
22.8	Czech GP, Brno	3rd	1st/FL
5.9	City of Imola GP, Imola	3rd	2nd
19.9	Valencia GP, Valencia	4th	8th
3.10	Australian GP, Phillip Island	7th	1st/FL
10.10	South African GP, Welkom	6th	1st/FL
24.10	Rio GP, Jacarepagua	2nd	1st/FL
31.10	Argentine GP, Buenos Aires	pole	3rd

Overall championship position: 1st

2000

500 World Championship

Bike: Nastro Azzurro Honda NSR500

Date	Event	Grid	Race
19.3	South African GP, Welkom	5th	DNF, crash/FL
2.4	Malaysian GP, Sepang	7th	DNF, crash
9.4	Japanese GP, Suzuka	13th	11th
30.4	Spanish GP, Jerez	2nd	3rd
14.5	French GP, Le Mans	10th	3rd/FL
28.5	Italian GP, Mugello	3rd	DNF/crash

11.6	Catalan GP, Catalunya	9th	3rd
24.6	Dutch GP, Assen	6th	6th
9.7	British GP, Donington Park	4th	1st
23.7	German GP, Sachsenring	6th	2nd
20.8	Czech GP, Brno	5th	2nd
3.9	Portuguese GP, Estoril	12th	3rd/FL
17.9	Valencia GP, Valencia	5th	DNF, crash
7.10	Rio GP, Jacarepagua	4th	1st/FL
15.10	Pacific GP, Motegi	5th	2nd/FL
29.10	Australian GP, Phillip Island	8th	3rd

Overall championship position: 2nd

2001

500 World Championship

Bike: Nastro Azzurro Honda NSR500

Date	Event	Grid	Race
8.4	Japanese GP, Suzuka	7th	1st
22.4	South African GP, Welkom	pole	1st/FL
6.5	Spanish GP, Jerez	pole	1st/FL
20.5	French GP, Le Mans	3rd	3rd
3.6	Italian GP, Mugello	pole	DNF, crash/FL
17.6	Catalan GP, Catalunya	pole	1st/FL
30.6	Dutch GP, Assen	3rd	2nd/FL
8.7	British GP, Donington Park	11th	1st/FL
22.7	German GP, Sachsenring	11th	7th
26.8	Czech GP, Brno	2nd	1st/FL
9.9	Portuguese GP, Estoril	3rd	1st
23.9	Valencia GP, Valencia	2nd	11th
7.10	Pacific GP, Motegi	4th	1st/FL
14.10	Australian GP, Phillip Island	2nd	1st
21.10	Malaysian GP, Sepang	2nd	1st/FL
3.11	Rio GP, Jacarepagua	5th	1st/FL

Overall championship position: 1st

2002

MotoGP World Championship

Bike: Repsol Honda RC211V

Date	Event	Grid	Race
7.4	Japanese GP, Suzuka	pole	1st/FL
21.4	South African GP, Welkom	pole	2nd
5.5	Spanish GP, Jerez	pole	1st/FL
19.5	French GP, Le Mans	pole	1st/FL
2.6	Italian GP, Mugello	pole	1st
16.6	Catalan GP, Catalunya	4th	1st/FL
29.6	Dutch TT, Assen	pole	1st/FL
14.7	British GP, Donington Park	pole	1st/FL
21.7	German GP, Sachsenring	6th	1st/FL
25.8	Czech GP, Brno	3rd	DNF, mech
8.9	Portuguese GP, Estoril	3rd	1st/FL
21.9	Rio GP, Jacarepagua	2nd	1st
6.10	Pacific GP, Motegi	6th	2nd
13.10	Malaysian GP, Sepang	8th	2nd
20.10	Australian GP, Phillip Island	7th	1st/FL
3.11	Valencia GP, Valencia	6th	2nd

Overall championship position: 1st

2003

MotoGP World Championship

Bike: Repsol Honda RC211V

Date	Event	Grid	Race
6.4	Japanese GP, Suzuka	pole	1st/FL
27.4	South African GP, Welkom	2nd	2nd/FL
11.5	Spanish GP, Jerez	5th	1st/FL
25.5	French GP, Le Mans	pole	2nd
8.6	Italian GP, Mugello	pole	1st
15.6	Catalan GP, Catalunya	pole	2nd/FL

28.6	Dutch TT, Assen	3rd	3rd
13.7	British GP, Donington Park	4th	3rd/FL
27.7	German GP, Sachsenring	4th	2nd
17.8	Czech GP, Brno	pole	1st/FL
7.9	Portuguese GP, Estoril	3rd	1st/FL
20.9	Rio GP, Jacarepagua	pole	1st
5.10	Pacific GP, Motegi	3rd	2nd/FL
12.10	Malaysian GP, Sepang	pole	1st/FL
19.10	Australian GP, Phillip Island	pole	1st/FL
2.11	Valencia GP, Valencia	pole	1st/FL

Overall championship position: 1st

2004

MotoGP World Championship

Gauloises Yamaha YZR-M1

Date	Event	Grid	Race
18.4	South African GP, Welkom	pole	1st
2.5	Spanish GP, Jerez	pole	4th
16.5	French GP, Le Mans	4th	4th
6.6	Italian GP, Mugello	3rd	1st
13.6	Catalan GP, Catalunya	2nd	1st
26.6	Dutch TT, Assen	pole	1st/FL
4.7	Rio GP, Jacarepagua	8th	DNF, crash
18.7	German GP, Sachsenring	2nd	4th
25.7	British GP, Donington Park	pole	1st
22.8	Czech GP, Brno	3rd	2nd
5.9	Portuguese GP, Estoril	2nd	1st/FL
19.9	Japanese GP, Motegi	3rd	2nd
2.10	Qatar GP, Losail	8th	DNF, crash
10.10	Malaysian GP, Sepang	pole	1st/FL
17.10	Australian GP, Phillip Island	2nd	1st
31.10	Valencia GP, Valencia	3rd	1st

Overall championship position: 1st

INDEX